SOCIAL SERVICE
AND THE
ART OF HEALING

SOCIAL SERVICE
AND THE
ART OF HEALING

BY

RICHARD C. CABOT, M.D.

Assistant Professor of Medicine in the Harvard Medical School
Assistant Visiting Physician at the Massachusetts General Hospital

NEW YORK

MOFFAT, YARD AND COMPANY

1915

NASW Classic Series

National Association of Social Workers
1425 H Street NW
Washington, D.C. 20005

International Standard Book No.: 0-87101-062-3

Library of Congress Catalog Card No.: 73-84257

Printed in the U.S.A. 1973

To the Social Workers of the Massachusetts General Hospital, whose fruitful labors this book lamely but most gratefully describes.

The author's thanks are due to the editors of *The Survey* and of *American Medicine* for permission to reprint portions of Chapters II and IV.

INTRODUCTION

THIS book is written to exemplify *three forms of team-work* which are now tending to ennoble medicine.

1. Social service—the modern type of what used to be called philanthropy—is drawing nearer and nearer to medicine. Public health and the extermination of disease,—that most fruitful cause of poverty, of misery, and of crime,—are the ideals for which doctors and social workers are joining hands to-day. When the doctor looks for the root-cause of most of the sickness that he is called upon to help, he finds social conditions, such as vice, ignorance, overcrowding, sweatshops, and poverty. When the social worker analyzes the reason why a family is in need, why a bread-winner is slack or shiftless,

why girls go wrong, and boys are caught stealing, he finds physical conditions, medical conditions—poor nutrition, bad air, alcoholism, tuberculosis, injuries in factories—staring him in the face.

Therefore *team-work of doctor and social worker* is called for, and the two professions are beginning to hear this call, to feel this kinship, and somewhat bashfully to work together.

2. But moral and spiritual problems also branch out of medical problems. Behind much physical suffering is the mental torment, the doubt, fear, worry, or remorse that the stress of life has created in most of the sick and in many who call themselves well. Without recognizing and treating these ills of the mind it is impossible to control the bodily sufferings for which people consult the doctor.

The doctor must be a psychologist, an educator, a physician to the whole man—body and soul alike. But can he?

Again *team-work* is the need. The doctor must work with the educator, the psychologist, and the minister as well as with the philanthropist. Only in this way can he become himself an educator, a teacher, putting the truth into his patients' minds and letting it do its own work there.

3. The problem of truth speaking *vs.* deception and concealment in medical practice springs naturally out of the newer educational and preventive work which is being recognized to-day as the core of medical helpfulness to the public as a whole. To fool a patient is tyranny, not guidance. He must understand what is being done for him if he is to do his part properly. This means *team-work of doctor and patient.*

To describe the changes just suggested whereby medical, social, and educational work are now being drawn together for the public good is the object of this book.

CONTENTS

SOCIAL SERVICE
AND THE
ART OF HEALING

SOCIAL SERVICE AND THE ART OF HEALING

CHAPTER I

BACKGROUNDS AND FOREGROUNDS IN MEDICAL WORK

THERE are two kinds of blindness from which I have suffered in my medical work. As I am now beginning to be convalescent, I note, with the sensibility of the recent sufferer, similar misfortunes in those around me. Blindness to what is before you just this minute and never before, or blindness to foregrounds, is a very common disease, due to the habit of looking off into the distance over the head (as it were) of the fact before you.

But there is another type of blindness in which the sufferer can see nothing ex-

cept the facts directly in front of his nose;
this I call blindness to backgrounds. I
will mention a group of examples of each
type.

I

In my medical work at the Massachusetts General Hospital I used to see about
30 patients a day, or 3,000 in my four
months' service. As I sit in my chair behind the desk, Abraham Cohen, of Salem
Street, approaches, and sits down to tell
me the tale of his sufferings; the chances
are ten to one that I shall look out of my
eyes and see, *not* Abraham Cohen, but *a
Jew;* not the sharp, clear outlines of this
unique sufferer, but the vague, misty com-
posite photograph of all the hundreds of
Jews who in the past ten years have shuf-
fled up to me with bent back and deprecat-
ing eyes, and taken their seats upon this
same stool to tell their story. I see a
Jew,—a nervous, complaining, whimper-
ing Jew,—with his beard upon his chest

and the inevitable dirty black frock-coat flapping about his knees. I do not see *this* man at all. I merge him in the hazy background of the average Jew.

I look behind, beyond, through this actual flesh-and-blood man, to my own habitual mental image of what I expect to see. Perhaps, if I am a little less blind than usual to-day, I may hear what he says instead of what I expect him to say. I may notice something in the way his hand lies on his knee, something that is queer, unexpected. That hand,—that hand, why, it's a muscular hand, it's a prehensile hand; and whoever saw a Salem Street Jew with a muscular hand before? That shocks me awake, at last. This is not merely "*a Jew*": this is a new kind of Jew. Why, his eyes are farther apart than I ever saw before in a Hebrew, and they don't avoid mine, but look straight at me with a long, deep look that somehow reminds me of the child in Raphael's Sistine Madonna.

They are blue eyes, thunder-cloud blue and very steady.

All this time he has been talking to me, not about himself, but about his fiancée whom I have examined and found consumptive yesterday. " Is she curable? " he asks, and " Would Colorado give her the best chance? How soon must she go,—before cold weather? Well, I think I can arrange it before that. I have a little business just established in Providence, but I think within a month I can sell it out, and take her to Denver or wherever is best."

" And what will you do out there? " I asked him. " Have you any friends to help you start in business? "

" Oh, I guess I'm strong enough to support two," he said. " I can work in the mines if there is nothing else." He saw nothing out of the way in giving up the retail dry-goods business which he had just got well under way in Providence, and going to work underground in the darkness of a mine, if there was any chance of saving his fiancée, the dried-up, mincing little milliner whom I had seen, or thought I'd seen, the day before. There was no certainty that he could save her. I told him that; but as soon as he understood that there was a chance, he was off to make his arrangements. He has gone now out into that unknown country, made, I hope, a little less forlorn and friendless to him by some letters I was able to give him to friends in Denver and Colorado Springs.

You could never forget that man if you had seen him,—his eyes, his quiet, slow voice, his muscular hands. I saw *him*. Yet he was no more real than the thousands of others whom I have seen and forgotten,—forgotten because I never saw *them,* but only their ghostly outline, their generic type, the racial background out of which they emerged.

The pity of it is that we see only what we have seen before. But the man, himself, is just precisely that which I have never seen before. So he is for me invisible: to him, as he sees himself, I am usually blind. I see a case of phthisis in a sad-eyed Irishman, but I cannot see, as he does, his children at home, the coldness of his employer when he asks if his job can be kept for him, the dreariness of this great hospital with its suggestion of nameless horrors behind doors which open for a moment and are swiftly closed again. The self that is pushing painfully through these experiences I fail to see, though it is all written in the stoop of his shoulders, the fear in his eyes, and the swift snatches of hesitating speech as he questions me about his lungs.

My students cannot even hear the new sound which I hear over one spot in his lungs,—a sound I never heard before. The students hear only the old common

sounds which every case of advanced
phthisis shows. These familiar old sounds
they promptly hear and record, but to
this new and startling sound, which might
be the prelude to a better understanding
of phthisis, they are deaf, though it is loud
and clear, *even to them,* after it is pointed
out to them.

It is very humiliating, this blindness to
the new facts, but it is a disease that we
all have in greater or less degree.

II

Let me tell you another of our humilia-
tions. This case of typhoid,—a " walking
typhoid " who has just turned up late,
near lunch time, at the Out-Patient Department, is obviously too sick to go home.
We must keep him in the hospital.
" Well, make out his recommendation slip,
and count his white corpuscles; ring for
John and the wheel-chair, and get his
clothes on, and don't forget to record the

dimensions of his spleen before you put his record slip away."

While these orders were being given, and while half a dozen assistants were executing them, a visitor to the hospital, not yet blinded and deafened by routine, heard the sick man ask three times for a drink of water. The visitor heard it: the others stood just as near, but none of them heard it. The sounds of his voice struck the tympanum of each man's ear, but to three of them it was an unusual request, and so was simply unheard; by two others it was heard, but disregarded, not because they were cruel-hearted,—not at all,—but because they were none of them assigned to *that* duty. It was no one's business in particular, and they all had other jobs— though, to be sure, jobs which could wait. One other assistant who heard the request said to himself, " Oh, he'll be in the ward in half an hour, and get plenty of cooler water; and what possible difference can

it make in his recovery anyhow? He'll
want water again in a few hours." So no
one stirred to get him the water until the
visitor could bear it no longer, and so
hunted up the tumbler and faucet, and
brought it himself. Goodness! to see the
sick man down that glass and look up
with the gleam of momentary relief was
something that visitor will never forget,
and wouldn't have missed for a year's life.

It was the foreground,—immediate,
pressing, *wholly transient* relief, *direct
personal* service of the simplest kind,—all
hidden from the minds of the regular assistants because they were looking off into
the distance, shaping the sufferer's future
course to the ward and towards recovery,
each pointing like a dog at his task, each
put in blinders, like a horse, by his concentration on the future and the distant.
All concentration is perilously near to
blindness outside the circle which is lit up
by the lamp of attention. The concen-

trated beam of the searchlight on a battle-
ship is typical of the mind of a busy, well-
trained, unimaginative man. Any well-
trained physician, as he looks with one eye
through a microscope, keeps the other eye
open, not closed, as the beginner does, but
wide open and *perfectly blind,* absolutely
unaware of the images that fall upon it.

So foregrounds always tend to be invisible to the man whose mind is elsewhere, intent upon its duties and its plans.

Sometimes an immediate crying need,
like that of the thirsty fever patient, is
disregarded, because, as we say, it is so
transient,—so momentary is the relief we
give. " He'll be thirsty again in half an
hour, and water won't cure him, anyway."
Yes. It is *now* and *here*. It does not
stretch into the distant future. In other
words, it is just what I have called it, a
foreground, and we are dreadfully prone
to forget that all eternity is made up of
half-hours as transient as this, as simple,

unimpressive, and insignificant as this. Nothing divine, nothing heroic, about this mean, commonplace present. If the occasion were imposing and resounding, we should rise to it nobly, but we notice nothing very important just here in this dingy laboratory or on that dreary corridor. We are almost indignant, if anyone tries to open our eyes. How can this piece of cheap, transient drudgery be linked to anything noble or significant?

" Lord, when saw we thee an hungered, or athirst, or a stranger, or naked, or sick, or in prison, and did not minister unto thee? "

Whatever we think, whatever our creeds say, our acts prove that we count it mere poetic exaggeration or literary figure when Christ said, " Inasmuch as ye did it not unto one of these least, ye did it not unto me." Christ said that every person, every moment, is a representative of the best in life,—a fair specimen opportunity.

"One of the great illusions is that the present hour is not the critical, decisive hour. God give me insight into to-day! The meal in the firkin, the milk in the pan, the ballad in the street, the glance of the eye, the form and gait of the body; show me the sublime presence lurking, as it always does lurk, in these suburbs and extremities of nature."

"Inasmuch as ye did it unto the least of these my brethren, ye did it unto me."

"What are you doing?"

"Oh, nothing. I have been doing that, I shall be doing so and so, but just now I am only"—"Inasmuch as ye did it not unto the *least* of these my brethren, ye did it not unto me."

III

From another point of view the duty of seeing the foreground becomes what Stevenson calls the *duty of happiness*. Not merely in some far-off divine event

which shall gloriously consummate and
fulfill the hopes of to-day, but all along
the road, in the details of meeting, serving,
directing our patients, in the very process
itself, and not only in its results, we must
find our happiness. Why must we? Because the man that doesn't enjoy his job
never does it well, and because, if you do
enjoy it, you will make others happy. If
it is only the fully achieved result that you
enjoy, you will be glum or grim most of
the time, for results are rare and uncer-
tain things, and the " best-laid plans of
mice and men gang aft agley." One ought
to enjoy the motion of walking down a
corridor, the actual questions and answers
by which we get at our patients' needs, the
simple technique of accurately reading a
thermometer and neatly recording the result on a chart. One ought to get pleasure
out of the eyes and faces, the gestures and
tones, of our patients and our fellow-
workers, the rich roll of the Scotchman's

brogue, the musical undulations of the Englishman's voice, and the quick, sympathetic flash of the Italian's eye. How stupid, how purblind, to front all these guests with the same stereotyped kindness, the same military precision, or, worst of all, the same dull inattention! Let us be in it! Let us catch the vital impulse of happiness that there is in sight, sound, and touch, in the infinite novelty and unexpectedness of the foreground.

This unique unforeseen opportunity, this direct personal service, this momentary joy springing from the sight and sound before us, make up a part of that foreground of our work to which I wish with all my heart I could never again be blind.

There is much else in that foreground of which I should like to speak. To be blind to the humor of the moment or to the pathos and the tragedy of the moment, to meet them all with the same engaging

smile or the same businesslike firmness,—
oh, it is a performance fit only for lay
figures on wheels! God grant we may act
to-morrow a little less like stuffed images!
No wise thought of the future, no deep
scientific ardor for the truth to be learned
from these sufferers, no preoccupation
with the wider interests of the community,
can justify our blindness to the here and
now.

IV

But I should wholly miss my mark if I
left you with the impression that I hate
blindness to foregrounds a whit less than
I hate the shortsightedness that can see
only the foreground.

We physicians are prone to scoff at the
habit of taking a drug for a symptom like
headache, without looking deeper to find
the underlying disorder of which this
headache is a symptom. We point out
very truly that only by finding and remov-
ing the cause of this headache—an eye-

strain, perhaps, or a stomach trouble—
can its recurrence be prevented and other
disorders nipped in the bud. This is as
it should be, but we need to carry the same
habit further. Why should we not push
on, and find out why this patient has the
stomach trouble? The headache is only a
symptom of stomach trouble, we say.
Yes, but the stomach trouble itself may
be only a symptom of chronic worry, and
the worry a symptom of deficient income.
The patient's expenses turn out to be a
trifle larger than his wages, and one of the
many bad results of this fact is the worry
that causes the stomach trouble, which in
turn causes the headache.

If we are really to treat that patient,
and not merely smother one of his symptoms under a dose of medicine, we must
push on into the background of his case,
and see what disease in the body politic—
perhaps in the organization of industry—
is behind his individual suffering. Not that

we should lose sight of him. On the contrary, we can do much better for him if, instead of stopping at the first stage, headache; or at the second stage, the stomach trouble; or even at the third, worry, we go into the matter of his income and outgo, and see if the two ends can't be made to meet. I have heard physicians giving advice to patients not to worry, advice that would be laughable if it were not so pathetic: " Just stop worrying " (you might just as well say stop breathing), " and take a long rest. Avoid all mental and physical strain." What his wife and children are to do meantime never occurs to this type of physician. The wife and children are in the background, out of range of his vision, and so for him they play no part in the case.

The shortsightedness of our hospitals in this respect is really marvelous. They will take in the wards a baby whose digestion is upset, give it free treatment, which costs the hospital twenty dollars, send it out again without any inquiry into the way the mother feeds it or the air it breathes or the clothes it wears. A month later the baby is back again, as sick as before, and from just the same causes. The hospital takes it again, spends another twenty dollars in getting it well, and so on. I followed up a case like this recently, and found that the mother was grossly ignorant of the first principles of feeding and caring for a baby, though perfectly capable of being taught. Even in terms of dollars and cents the hospital is losing by its blindness to backgrounds. The same ailments in the same patients are treated again and again, with a wisdom equal to that of the sage who dipped up water with a sieve.

Our patients shoot by us like comets, crossing for a moment our field of vision, then passing out into oblivion. At the end of hundreds of hospital records one can

read the words " Discharged well," and
the eminent surgeon figuring up his " suc-
cesses," often counts as such all who have
left the hospital well, and never been heard
from again. But peer into the background a little, follow up these cases for a
few months or years, and you will often
find that " the last state of that man was
worse than the first." The past and the
future of our cases is one aspect of that
background of their lives to which we are
so blind.

v

Another background of our experience
with the sick, and one to which we are
almost as blind as we are to their home
conditions, is the moral and spiritual set-
ting from which their physical symptoms
project into our foreground. This is the
field in which our friends the Mental Heal-
ers and Christian Scientists have worked
with so much success. Mind Cure and
Christian Science have a strong hold upon

thousands in this community to-day because they have not been blind to the
spiritual background of physical suffering. Doctors and nurses used to be un-
willing to admit that *fear* causes disease
because the Mind Curists have so long
said that it did, but now there is scarcely
a week in which you will fail to find upon
several of the record slips in our Out-
Patient Department the diagnosis, *"Ap-
prehension."*

A man comes to us complaining of a trifling pain in his chest, but also sleepless,
without appetite, losing weight, too weak
to work,—all because the trifling pain
happens to be in the spot where he has been
told his heart is. I examine his heart, find
it wholly normal, tell him so with all the
emphasis I can express, and add that he
couldn't die if he tried, will probably live
to be a hundred, and that meantime he
must go to work and put the idea of heart
trouble out of his head once for all. In

three days that man will be a changed
being. You will hardly recognize him as
the same. He believed me because he
heard me tell the patient just ahead of
him that he *had* heart trouble, and could
never hope to work again. Believing me,
he began to sleep and eat, to work, to love
life, and to throw from his shoulders the
millstone of fear that had been weighing
him down.

Every candid physician knows that fear
causes some disorders, that self-absorption
causes others, that sin and half-smothered
remorse cause still others. But he is
afraid to admit the full consequences of
these truths. Because he knows that cancer, typhoid, meningitis, are *not* caused by
fear or by sin, because he fears to admit
that the Mind Curists have a piece of real
truth in their possession, he blinds himself
to this whole realm of fact. He calls it
rubbish or sentimentality or superstition
or simple ignorance, but he has to recog-

nize it more or less in his practice, though grudgingly.

The enormous influence of spiritual environment, of friendship, of happiness, of beauty, of success, of religion, is grievously, ludicrously underestimated by most physicians, nurses, and hospital superintendents. There are diseases that cannot be cured without friendship, patients that never will get well unless you can get them to make a success of something or to conquer their own self-absorption by a self-devotion, losing their life to find it.

Our blindness to backgrounds of this type is well illustrated by the recent remark of a hospital superintendent: " I want you to understand," he said,—to someone who was laboring to correct some of the results of our habitual blindness to backgrounds—" I want you to understand that we want sense, and not sentiment, in this work." Think of the short-

sightedness of one who has lived for years
in the midst of these problems,—your
problems and mine,—yet doesn't know
that *both* sense and sentiment are absolutely essential in any competent medical
work. It is as if one should say, " We
want eyes, but no ears, in this work."

VI

Another type of blindness to backgrounds, and one less appealing perhaps
to most of us, is the blindness to the scientific truth which can and ought to be won
out of every case of poverty, ignorance,
or disease. Now, I hope you will not
suspect me of lack of respect for the humanitarian side of medicine, the direct
immediate helpfulness of man to man,—
in short the foreground. But I wonder
if we all realize that Pasteur, who had
scarcely any direct dealings with patients,
scarcely entered what I call the foreground of medical work, won truth that

has been the means of saving more lives, more suffering, more rack and ruin in human flesh, than all the doctors and nurses and social workers now living. It is the man of science who works out the prevention of typhoid epidemics, banishes yellow fever from Cuba and the terrible parasitic anemia from Porto Rico. You and I can only alleviate a little suffering here and there. We are pygmies of human helpfulness compared to those giants who look beyond and behind the sick patient in the foreground, to the tiny glimpse of truth in the far distance, and work towards that distant gleam by faith. I want to make you feel as I do the spiritual nobility of scientific work. It deals almost exclusively with the unseen. You and I deal with the seen, with the ills and griefs of the foreground, and we are quite right in doing so, but we ought to give all honor to the spiritual imagination by means of which the man of science grasps those un-

seen truths which are eternal, and, using
them as a lever, lifts us all out of our difficulties. Let me illustrate.

It was a mere idea, a mere theory, for
which Lazear laid down his life five years
ago in Cuba,—the theory that mosquitoes
transmitted yellow fever from man to
man. Nothing visible, nothing reliable
and certain in it. To test it, men must be
found who would allow themselves to be
bitten by mosquitoes which had previously
bitten a yellow-fever patient. Lazear and
three other physicians were bitten, and by
their example induced several others (sol-
diers in the American army) to do the
same. All were infected, all took yellow
fever. The theory was proved, and Lazear died. To-day, and as a direct result
of the scientific work that culminated in
the sacrifice of Lazear's life, Cuba is free
from yellow fever after one hundred and
fifty years of the scourge.

Those doctors did not directly serve

any patient.   They nursed no one, they carried no cup of cold water.   In books and laboratories they imagined, thought out, worked out, and proved that theory.   As we look back now from the solid ground of assured fact, with New Orleans saved three years ago from decimation owing to the application of this theory, it is hard to realize the imagination, the faith, the hold upon the unseen, which went to the elaboration of that theory.   " Faith," says Saint Paul, " is the substance of things hoped for, the evidence of things not seen."

You would realize the high spiritual quality of this work if you were associated with the men who do it.   Do you remember Scott's description of the Roundheads in " Old Mortality,"—the lean, bare-headed group upon the hill, utterly wanting in the graces and trappings of the Cavaliers, poor and mean, silent, unworldly, shining only by the inner light of their determined purpose and of their abounding faith in the unseen?

That is the type evolved by scientific discipline, a discipline the full rigor of which must be experienced to be appreciated. If ever you feel inclined to belittle the work of scientific men, or to believe the legends of their brutality and materialism, go and look into the faces of any gathering of them, and listen to their work. I think you will be convinced, as I am, that no small part of the seed of the God-fearing Puritans has taken root and is flourishing in the rigorous asceticism of the modern scientific investigator. We accept the fruits of his labors, and live on them like parasites, but we do not often stop to acknowledge our indebtedness, still less to realize that the work has been done by minds disciplined by a degree of self-denial, a degree of renunciation of the world and its rewards, before which you and I should quail.

VII

I have set foreground and background apart, and described them separately, as if it were true that the more one sees of the one, the less the other is visible. But, of course, that is not so. The man who has a clear sense of the individuality and sacredness of each person and each moment of time will yet run into confusion and distortion unless he backs his foreground view with the vista of the distant, the past and the future, the background of the community life out of which this individual has emerged and to which he belongs. The only justice to one individual is justice to all. The only true consideration of one is consideration of all.

The humanitarian and the scientific sides of our work need each other as man and woman do. Science without humanity becomes arid and, finally, discouraged.

Humanity without science becomes scrappy and shallow.

No one ought to be satisfied to test his work by any easier standards than these:

First. Am I seeing all the actual facts, the ever-new and unique facts, the crying and immediate needs as they come before me?

Second. Am I tracing out as far and as deep as I can the full bearing, the true lesson, the unseen spirit of this moment, this situation, this calamity, this illness?

Am I using my eyes and ears, my sympathies and my imagination, as hard as I can? Am I searching for the deepest meaning, the widest bearing, the furthest connection of these facts? Am I seeing and helping as truly as I can the foreground and the background of my work?

CHAPTER II

THE NATURE OF SOCIAL WORK, ESPECIALLY IN ITS RELATION TO MEDICINE

As soon as we open our eyes to the *backgrounds of medical work* such as I exemplified in the last chapter, social, educational, and preventive activities begin to loom up round us in deep vistas which we cannot reasonably refuse to explore. A man is not flat like a card. We cannot get the whole of him spread out upon our retina at once. The bit of him which is recorded in the history of his aches, his jumps, and his weaknesses is built into the rest of his life and character like a stone in an arch. To change any part of him appreciably we must change the whole. As well might one try to pick up a man's shadow and carry it away as to treat his

physical ills by themselves without knowledge of the habits that so often help to
make him sick and the character of which
these habits are the fruit.

Yet physicians and hospital managers
have only just begun to realize this
because the inquiry into the ultimate
causes and results of disease has not yet
gathered much momentum. The question:
" Why does this disease occur at all? " is
still thought of as one which a few paid
officials or virtuous amateurs may well be-
stir themselves to answer, provided they
have the time and provided they do it without disturbing the practical work of the
busy physician. The average practitioner
is used to seeing his patients flash by him
like shooting stars—out of darkness into
darkness. He has been trained to focus
upon a single suspected organ till he thinks
of his patients almost like disembodied
diseases.

" What is there in the waiting-room? "

I asked my assistant as I arrived one morning at the hospital.

" A pretty good lot of material," said he briskly. " There's a couple of good hearts, a big liver with jaundice, a floating kidney, three pernicious anæmias, and a flatfoot."

Among such flying fragments as these the physician has to pass his days. He couldn't earn a living if he did not attend first and chiefly to the part that is thrust before him. He must clip very close the wings of his curiosity as to the " *whence* " and the " *whither* " of these apparitions.

When a bloody finger is presented to him for relief he looks far enough to see that it is attached to an arm and the arm to a body of average shape and carriage. Beyond that he cannot afford to look. The finger waits for attention. His work calls. He cannot be looking off into space for causes and results. He must get busy, and as he does so a mist settles down along these puzzling vistas. Those who have time can ask "how it happened." That is not his business, for the accident must be attended to however it happened. The finger must be dressed whoever owns it; and as soon as it is bandaged and splinted, there's a boil to be opened, a sprain to be examined, some ether to be given, and so on through a day, a week, a year. Brief, isolated arcs in the span of a human life, accidents, fragments, each crowding out the last—never a whole, a finished day, or a story completed—that's the doctor's life, as it tends to be—tends with all the strength of the pressure brought to bear on him by a public hungry for immediate relief,—any relief, "but be quick about it," and by the need to earn a living and support a family in decent comfort.

If disease were mostly *" accident "* and "hard luck" or "too bad" as we are prone consolingly to assure one another that it is, my plea would be nonsense and

this book would never have been written.
If sickness usually fell from the clouds
and floored man like the lightning stroke
there would be no use in hunting for ultimate causes in the victim's character, inheritance or environment, no sense in prat-
ing of social or educational work in connection with the healing art.   It is because
the sphere of accident is becoming more
and more contracted that the importance
of social, psychical, and educational causes
looms up larger and larger every year.
Disease is not often " hard luck " nor " too
bad."   For the most part it is as bad as we
—the tax-payers—allow it to be and as we
—the unconquerable soul of us—recognize
it to be.   *Preventable disease* stares us in
the face.   Yet still the rank and file of the
medical profession are too busy with *cases*
of disease (*a " case " means an accident*)
to have time for *causes*.   It is only when
the social workers stir us into action
that the Anti-Tuberculosis crusade and

the Clean Milk crusade, the Pure Food
law, the Playground Association, and the
School Hygiene agitation come into being.

Why, then, does not the social worker
get the credit that he deserves from all of
us, physicians, parents, and citizens, who
have reason to thank him for the most and
the best of public health work and preventive medicine?

Why is it that lawyers, business men,
" hard-headed " people generally look
upon the social worker as belonging " mid-
way between the dancing master and the
theologian "—among the luxuries and the
trifles, the dreams and impracticalities?

I believe the answer is found in the fact
that social work *as a profession* is new. It
has evolved out of more or less haphazard
alms-giving and spasmodic benevolence,
out of Utopian philanthropy and priestly
" good works." The motives, the efforts,
and (here and there) the superbly effective practice of social work,—all this

is ancient and tolerably familiar; but the organization of these efforts into a definite profession, trained, paid, and recognized like engineering, medicine, or law, is a matter of hardly more than a decade.

Even now I think the value of the social worker and his proper recognition are considerably limited by the fact that he cannot often recognize himself or tell you what the value of his profession is. He is an expert. But *in what is he an expert?* What is his special field of knowledge and of skill?

I want in this chapter to attempt an answer to this question because I think that the public will not get the best service either out of doctors, or out of social workers, until the close relationship of these two professions is generally recognized.

In my opinion, medical and social workers must act together as a team, if they are to serve the public efficiently. But this they cannot do till they recognize and the public recognizes their affinity.

I

What is Social Work?

" Philanthropy " and " charity " are its poor but honest parents. From their point of view we may naturally approach its definition—beginning with negatives.

(a) We may assume in the first place that, in the evolution of the conception of philanthropy, we have left behind the stage at which a fair sample of the morning's work was the round of visits made by the rich and kindly lady, with her basket of choice victuals, virtuously dispensed to her beneficiaries, " the poor." We no longer need to expose and refute the twin delusions:

That philanthropy is especially meritorious work.

That philanthropy is easy, provided our motives are good.

To-day we all abhor the patronizing attitude in theory, if not always in practice,
and we have had it effectually brought
home to us that it is hard to do good and
easy to do harm in social work.

It is never safe to suppose that a stage
of growth which we have left behind us
is, therefore, to be dropped bodily out
of our theory and our practice. There
is a good in that old " I am better than
thou " attitude; truth in the *de haut en bas*
treatment of the social sufferer;—what
good, what truth, I shall try to indicate
later in my address.

(b) But the error and harm of these
methods are more obvious than the truth of
them. Stung by this fact, philanthropists
have striven in the next stage of evolution
to democratize social work. " Not alms,
but a friend," becomes our motto, as we
come to recognize that by the giving of
money, food, and clothes we can easily do
harm, while much more often, by the giv-

ing of friendly advice, sympathy, and encouragement, or simply by "lending a hand," we may be of use. Realizing that anyone who is being treated coldly, as an inferior, an outcast, and an opportunity for the "acquisition of merit," is not likely to get any good out of the transaction, we try to make our common humanity a meeting ground on which we may do some service. "Not alms, but a friend."

But this second conception of charity as simple friendliness is also becoming outgrown. It is good as far as it goes, but there are two obvious flaws in it:

First, wise friends, skillful, experienced, and foresighted friends, are rare, and any other kind of friends may be useless or worse in the difficult tasks of social work. Mere friendliness will not do. "Friendly visiting" is a term as applicable to the physician's work as to the philanthropist's. Both make friendly visits: each also does his own more specific service.

Second, friends are not made in a day or a month. The skilled social worker may, in the end, succeed in becoming the friend of those who need his help, but in the long intervening time which must elapse before genuine friendship emerges, we must have some spiritual *modus vivendi,* some reason other than friendship, other than friendliness, for meeting at all. The attitude in which one person regularly gives and seldom receives help, the one-sided relation, is not friendship and tends only very slowly to the growth of friendship. I take it that all of us are glad to to see that the word " friendship " is coming to be less lightly used, that we are more conscious of the rarity and sacredness of the relation, and of the time, patience, and rare good fortune necessary for its creation. Letters to perfect strangers beginning, " My dear friend," are, I hope, less common than they used to be. The following extract from the Boston Directory of Charities was written in 1899 and remained unchanged until 1906, though it has been expunged in the edition now current:

" Personal friendship furnished to both sexes and all ages " [by a certain charitable society!]

The wholesale acquisition of " friends " by the dozen a week is going out of fashion.

Where, then, shall we look for that spiritual standing-ground on which the social worker may meet those who need his help, without a patronizing air, but also without blaspheming the sacred name of friend? Is such a standing-ground already anywhere in use? Where shall we look to find pleasant, healthy, manly, democratic relationships maintained between persons differing sharply in inheritance, education, habits, and environments, between rich and poor, wise and ignorant, cultivated and uncultivated?

(c) We may answer with Mr. Brackett, head of the School for Social Workers in Boston, that we find the ideal standing-ground in the *neighborly relationship.* When neighbors meet in country villages, at church suppers, town meetings, and cattle shows, we have friendly, comfortable, democratic relations between many sorts and conditions of men, without great intimacy, but equally without any snobbishness.

Can we extend this neighborliness to cover the relationship between a professional social worker and those in need of his advice? I think not; the two are not neighbors in any ordinary sense. They have not the common property-interests, common acquaintances, common dealings in town, church, and club affairs, that make the stable basis of true neighborliness and furnish topics of conversation. The settlement worker may persuade himself not only that he really has these com-

mon interests with his neighbors, but that
this fact makes the basis of his relationship to them more natural and more effective than that of any other social workers.
But I think that it is more and more
agreed that valuable as settlement work
surely is, the relationship is not essentially
that of neighbor to neighbor, but of
teacher to pupil or pupil to teacher. The
settlement worker rarely brings up his
family at the settlement, and in his relations to those who are literally his neighbors he is more like the explorer, or the
lighthouse keeper. He is not there for
the same reason that any of the people in
the adjoining houses are there, any more
than the explorer is in the jungle for the
same reason as the bushranger and the
antelope.

The most valuable work which the settlement worker does is not, I think, as
neighbor but as investigator, teacher, expert interpreter, and referee. Still more

obviously, but no more genuinely, is this
true of other social workers.

To fall back on the scriptural usage of
the words " my neighbor " is to confuse
the issue, for that phrase, like " friendliness," defines everybody's business in general and not the social worker's in particular. Everyone is, in the scriptural sense,
the neighbor of all with whom he is
brought into contact. But everyone is
not a social worker either in fact or in
ideal. Neither my neighbor in space nor
my neighbor in scripture, nor any attempt
to fuse the two meanings, furnishes the
central idea of social work. It is something much more definite than this. Yet
we see in the attempts to think of the social
worker first as a friend and later as a
neighbor the natural and proper reaction
against the aristocratic and patronizing
idea of charity alluded to at the beginning.

The " Lady Bountiful " conception of

charity accented unduly and perversely
the perfectly true fact that the giver is *in
some respect* the superior of the recipient.
The conception of social work as a relationship between friends and neighbors
errs equally on the other side, for it sup-
presses the difference and proclaims that
the unity is all in all. Both conceptions
are true, both one-sided. What can unite
them? Modern social work answers:

The conception of expert service.

(d) Here, I think, is the solution of the
problem of distinctions within a democracy. This is the immortal soul of the
patronizing conception of charity, surviv-
ing the death of its body. Superiority
there is and ought to be, but superiority
in one respect—the obvious superiority of
the expert. We can look up to the expert
with ready acknowledgment of his superiority. We are not his equal here, but there
is not a particle of sense of shame on the
one side or of condescension on the other.

As we sit by the stage driver, or travel with the Adirondack guide, the motorman, or the navigator, our relationship is perfectly democratic because each tacitly acknowledges the other as an expert in his own line, giving and receiving respect, and, if there is opportunity, exchanging information such as to strengthen each other's weak points.

This is the nearest approach to ideal democracy outside the neighborhood relationship. Whenever the neighborhood relationship does not genuinely exist, this relationship of mutually acknowledged experts is the best alternative.

A third, slightly different but equally democratic relationship is exemplified in the relationship of a public school teacher to a child in her class, or of a physician to some of the more ignorant of his patients. Here there is expert knowledge on one side and none on the other. The common ground of meeting is the common interest in the subject studied or in the health sought. This makes something approaching a neighborhood relationship, the essence of which is a common interest in property, in business, in town, church, or club affairs. It differs from the neighborhood relation in that the meeting ground is in thought and in hope instead of in the neighborhood interests. Teacher and pupil are both interested in the subjects studied; doctor and patient are united in the pursuit of health. On these grounds they meet.

There are, as far as I know, no satisfying human ties except:

(a) Family relationships and friendship;

(b) Neighborhood relationships;

(c) Relationships based on common interests (financial, scientific, artistic, athletic, etc.) ;

(d) Relationships between experts, and

(e) Relationships of the teacher and pupil type.

Now the social worker cannot often be a professional friend, a professional " uncle " or " aunty," a professional neighbor, or a professional " good man.". Nor can he often share in the financial, artistic, political, or scientific interests of his client. Hence the social worker must take one of the parts that are left. He must hold his position and command respect as an expert, as a teacher, or as a pupil.

He needs all the virtues no more and no less than the railroad man, the farmer, or the shopkeeper. But his first and chief duty to all men is to give, with such ripening sympathy and friendliness as is possible under the circumstances, the benefit of his expert skill, and so fulfill his special function in the community.

In a general way, I think, this view is coming to prevail. The social worker has more and more, in the last decade, come to command respect and salary as an expert. People are beginning to take this view of him, and with the change come the new schools for social workers, which plan not only to inspire their members with social ardor, but to give them the professional knowledge and the rigorous training necessary for the difficult and delicate task which they have undertaken.

But this attitude is new and not yet very stable. The social worker has not yet won the position or the salary that he deserves, because the public rightly demands that a genuine expert shall be expert in something in particular; if we are to acknowledge his preëminence we must have some clear idea of what it consists in.

We are told by Mr. Edward T. Devine that many topics, many sciences, group themselves about the study of philanthropy. Political economy, housekeeping, law, medicine, public hygiene, architecture, statistics, the humanities, all form, he says, more or less important auxiliaries. But what is their center? Can we say that the general purpose to do good, the general aim of *social amelioration,* is definite enough to constitute such a center? I think not. For that should be everyone's business and no one profession should have a monopoly of it. It is too all-inclusive.

On the other hand, *the proper adminis-tration or withholding of financial relief* is too narrow, for social workers deal with many persons who are not dependent and ask for no relief. We need as the center and focus of social work something more comprehensive than relief but less vague than charity or neighborliness or the at-tempt to serve the public good; we need a center around which we can group the auxiliary topics and sciences. What is that center?

A comparison with medical work may

help us here.   The physician, like the social worker, finds it necessary to master the rudiments of many sciences in which he cannot hope to become an expert.   He dips into chemistry, optics, physiology, biology, and ethics, but he does not merely organize these sciences for the physical good of man.   He arranges them about a central core of knowledge, a central science, which occupies more than half of all his training,—the *diagnosis and treatment of disease*.   It is only in this field that he is an expert.

Do social workers possess already any such central body of knowledge to which all the rest of their studies contribute?   In point of fact I think the most valuable social workers do use such a science in practice, though rarely in clear consciousness.   But it seems as if the schools of philanthropy had lagged behind the workers, because these schools conceive their functions to be fulfilled by teaching a little of the auxiliary sciences, such as house-keeping, hygiene, and political economy, while spending most of their time on a bird's-eye view of the existing agencies and institutions which have been created as remedies for the difficulties which confront us.

But the successful social worker often knows very little of political economy, medicine, and the rest. He differs from the rest of us in quite other respects. Another man may know more of all these sciences than the social worker and yet be a bungler in the actual craftsmanship of social work. He may have a good working knowledge of all the items in the directory of charities, of all the existing agencies for the cure of social ills, and yet make an utter mess of it when he tries to do a bit of probation work or to pull up a shiftless family.

This (some will say) is because he has not inherited or acquired the unteachable

tact, the actual deftness in handling cases
which the successful worker possesses.
He must first be born to it, we say, and
then half-instinctively find out the rest as
he gets his experience in the work itself.
But this is equally true of the diagnosis
and treatment of disease, or the appreciation and interpretation of music. The doctor and the musician, as well as the social
worker, must be born for his profession,
else he cannot be trained for it. But we
do train him despite the old false antith-
esis, "born, not made."

The central knack and talent of the social worker, then, is not economics, or
neighborliness, or a general desire for social
amelioration, nor is it something unteachable. The essence and center of social
work, that which corresponds to diagnosis
and treatment as the center of the group
of medical sciences, I may venture to
phrase as:

The study of character under adversity

*and of the influences that mold it for good
or ill.*

This is the genuinely new science which
it is the business of our best social students
to build up in theory, where it already exists more or less concisely and satisfac-
torily in practice. In social work the art
has preceded the science, as it did in medicine and music; but neither science nor
art can live well without the other.
The science must back and direct the
art.

In support of this, which is the central
thesis of this chapter, I shall adduce two
groups of arguments:

First, illustrations of the fact that successful social workers are now engaged,
for the most part, in the practice of this
art, the diagnosis and treatment of character under adversity, which I am urging
should be systematically taught in schools
of philanthropy.

Second, reasons for believing that it is

not impossible to teach this science, nor inconceivable to make a text-book about it.

II

Taking up the first of the above theses, I will remind you, first of all, of the wide, and interesting field of *probation work*. When I first became a director of the Boston Children's Aid Society and began to spend time with the paid agents of the Society, I watched them in their advisory and supervisory work with children and their parents. I soon became aware that I was witnessing the expert practice of the art of character-study and character-molding. Mr. C. W. Birtwell, Mr. W. H. Pear, and Mr. S. C. Lawrence, with whom I was chiefly associated, went at their cases with a definite diagnostic method, studied their antecedents, their environment, their present characteristics, their strong points, their weak points, and their possibilities with as scientific and sure-footed a course of procedure in their *mental* diagnosis as the physician uses in his much simpler *physical* diagnosis.

First diagnosis, then treatment. Knowing the child's environment, his diet, his play, his school, his parents, his companions, his amusements, where he is weak and where he is strong, how his strength and his weakness are linked, and where these links can be unfastened, these experts in the psychology of erring children proceeded to choose a remedy among the resources of the community. They used clubs, churches, country families for placing out, personal supervision at home, the help of a properly assisted and directed parent, studying and judging these agencies of the environment as molders of character, i.e., as spiritual influences.

Questions of financial relief and dependence are here quite subordinate. If we define the vocation of the social worker as the diagnosis and treatment of financial distress (as has been suggested to me) we should have to say that such probation work was not social work at all, because it is in most cases a labor of education pure and simple. What is the weakness in this child's character; how can it be helped? Environment is, of course, most carefully studied, but not only the physical environment. The influences about the child and their bearing on his character are the chief subjects of the social worker's study when he has made his diagnosis and turns to treatment.

Take as a second example the care of the girls placed out from a large reform school like that at Lancaster, Mass. Even a slight acquaintance with the young women who are in charge of these girls makes one at once aware of the same trained management of character based on the skillful study of character in its environment. Which girl is in trouble because of excess of vitality, and which because of moral

flabbiness, deficient vitality? Which one
is really below par mentally, which is in
need chiefly of encouragement and a
healthy spiritual environment? Character is always the central problem, the
true basis both of classification and of the
choice of remedies. To classify these girls
according to their " crimes " has only a
very limited value and cannot be used as
a sufficient basis for intelligent treatment.

Here, again, there is often no question
of charity or of financial relief. In many
if not most of these cases there is no financial or economic question at issue. The
problems are mental, moral, and physical.

Is it so different in the work of charity
organizations and in the treatment of persons who are financially dependent? As
I watch the work of experts in this field
I feel, as in other instances, that the task
is chiefly one of delicate and difficult
psychical diagnosis and psychical treatment. To the expert social worker an

application for relief comes as a complaint of pain does to the physician. It is a symptom of deeper defects. *Poverty is to social work as pain is to medical work.* It may or may not need treatment, but thorough diagnosis is the first necessity. To find out whether it is discouragement, overwork, unforeseeable misfortune, arrogance, conceit, forgetfulness, unimaginativeness, congenital degeneracy, alcoholism, ignorance, or some other cause that is back of the financial breakdown,— this is what I see these experts busy about.

Next they ask: What sound life, what untainted character, is left, and what is the best that can be made of it? What influences can be brought to bear on the paralyzed will, the spasmodic and ungoverned energies, the darkened and narrowed mental horizon? Physical and financial diagnosis, physical and financial remedies are always useful, but always subordinate to the central problem, which is more like a problem in horticulture than one in economics.

Even in the almshouse, where we should be dealing, I take it, chiefly with the wrecks and relics of character, our problem is still how to make the most and best of what life and character is left; how to prevent it from degenerating into a merely brutal or vegetable existence; how to make the outlook less gloomy and desperate.

Another evidence that character study is behind most if not all of the common relief problems appears when we ask: Why do we allow many widows and children, and most that are sick or aged, to be dependent? Why do we not urge them all on into the ranks of the self-supporting? Some children, many women, and a certain number of sick or aged men are doubtless the better for earning their salt; others are not. The principle of decision, which seems to be recognized by expert social workers, is this: What is best for the individual's development and for the community? It is not good for the mental and moral life of *most* healthy adults to be dependent financially or in any other way. Whenever we find exceptions to this rule they must be made because we believe it best for the character of the individuals and of the community in which they live that they should be financially dependent in order that they may put forth their full powers in ways not now remunerative; for example, in getting educated or getting well. But some children, some sick, and some old people ought nevertheless to work for a living. Why? Because they need it to keep their souls alive, and because nothing else will do this as far as we know. Our campaign is not against all poverty and distress but against *such* poverty and distress as cramp the normal development of character.

The fact that dependence and relief are usually, but not always, undesirable in the

healthy adult, that they are more often
desirable in children under sixteen and in
the sick, while in adolescence dependence
is sometimes good and sometimes bad,
shows that even in that portion of social
work that deals with relief problems, the
underlying question, in many if not in
most cases, must be still: What is the
structure and need, the strength and weakness, of these persons before us, and what
is the effect on them and on the community
of the dependence which we propose to
create or to abolish?

I have now considered the psychical
factor in social work as exemplified in the
case of misbehaving children, adolescents,
and adult dependents.   In the charities
aiding unmarried mothers, the blind, the
feeble-minded, in the training of social
secretaries, welfare workers, settlement
workers, prison officials, home and school
visitors, school nurses, factory nurses,
tuberculosis nurses, and workers in church

clubs, it is even more obvious that not relief but the analysis and understanding of character under adversity, and of the means of developing it, are the main things to be learned.

I will rest at this point my case for the thesis that *the true business of the social worker is psychical diagnosis and treatment,* a labor parallel to that of the physical diagnosis and treatment of the physician.

III

But now, granting that this is the sort of wisdom to be desired and striven for, is it possible to teach it? What has been done thus far towards reducing it to teachable, that is, to scientific form?

Character and the influences molding it,—this is the subject of our inquiry. The studies relating to it can be arranged in two groups:

1. The researches of Jacob Riis, Helen

Bosanquet, Jane Addams, Robert Woods, and others, into *the psychology of the hard-pressed*. Put a newly-arrived immigrant into a crowded tenement house district among races and customs foreign to him—what results? The outcome of this huge laboratory experiment is reported in such books as Jane Addams's " Newer Ideals of Peace," Riis's " How the Other Half Lives," Woods's " The City Wilderness " and " Americans in Progress."

Put a relatively homogeneous race into the crowded capital of a small and crowded island, squeeze it between the upper and nether millstones of poverty and drink: what type of character results? Mrs. Bosanquet has answered the question in a series of searching and skillful studies.[1]

Charles Booth's monumental survey of London conditions (" Life and Labor in London "; 8 volumes) and especially the

[1] " The Family," " Rich and Poor," " The Standard of Life," " The Strength of the People."

recent " Pittsburg Survey " are concerned throughout with the bearing of physical and economic conditions on character, though the connection is not always thoroughly worked out.

2. The second group of studies is less generally known to social workers themselves and has been carried on for the most part by their cousins the educators. I refer to the child-study researches. Like the last group, these investigations deal with character in its environment, but here the emphasis is on character—there, on environment. These character-studies are supposedly concerned with normal children, but as all children are more or less faulty, the distinction from those who come into the field of the social worker is not a sharp one. Indeed, the distinction between the vocation of the educator and that of the social worker should be merely one of convenience.

Without trying to sum up in any way

the work of the child-study researches, I
have selected two interesting items in illustration of the sort of study which I hope
to see much furthered in schools for social
workers.

Joseph Lee [1] has made a striking effort
to found a character-study of children, by
dividing them into three ages, with special
reference to play:

(a) The "dramatic" age, when the
child is fond of plays of make-believe;

(b) The "Big-Injun" period, when
he is prone to individualistic, realistic occupations;

(c) The "age of loyalty," when team-
work becomes possible.

Professor Josiah Royce, of Harvard
University, gave some years ago a course
of lectures on the character of children, lectures containing a few references to children's faults and their management.
After each lecture he was bombarded with

[1] Joseph Lee: *Educational Review.* December, 1900.

interesting questions from anxious mothers and teachers, who were hungry for such crumbs of a science of the diagnosis and treatment of children's faults as were dropped in a course of lectures not concerned primarily with these questions.

The attempted classification at the Lancaster Reform School for girls by the characteristics supposed to lead to the crime rather than by the crime itself is another straw floating on the same current. I will merely mention also Mrs. Bosanquet's [1] studies in the mental characteristics of the shiftless, and President Hadley's [2] division of the college students into men of action, men of literary interests (artistic), and men of science.

These disjointed scraps and suggestions are, of course, no proof that a science of character-study and character-molding

[1] Helen Bosanquet: " Aspects of the Social Problem," page 83.

[2] A. T. Hadley: *Harper's Magazine*, June, 1905.

exists. The *art* exists, but the *science* has not yet gotten very far. I have often longed to have the opportunity to transcribe, like some sort of a Boswell, the wisdom, the science, which I know is stored in the minds and active in the habits of our most skillful social workers but is nowhere in print. When these experts die much wisdom will die with them. There is, however, especially in France, some scientific work on this matter, work with which I think social workers should be more familiar.

Social workers have already begun to get in touch with psychotherapeutic literature on the one hand and with psychodiagnostic literature on the other. But the acquaintance should ripen into intimacy. Social workers are constantly confronted with the problem of training the will, but how many of them have ever seen J. Payot's book on the " Education of the Will," or Levy's monograph on the same subject, or even

Dubois's "Psychic Treatment of Nervous Disease"? These books are not exhortations or theoretical analyses. They are the works of men who have been training wills,—more or less diseased and broken wills,—and report their methods and the degree of success that can be reasonably expected.

We all agree that the treatment of cases as they come to us must not be mechanical or routine. If we are to avoid this we must distinguish the types of character with which we are concerned and adapt our methods accordingly. But do social workers ever read Fouillée's "Temperament and Character,—Their Variations According to Race, Sex, and Individuality," [1] or Levy's "Psychology of Character," or Paulhan's works on the same subject? As a matter of fact, I think social workers can write books far better than these. They are more closely in touch

[1] Paris (Alcan), 108 Boulevard St. Germain, 1895.

with the facts. They treat more cases than these writers do. Yet these books will be found stimulating, unless I am very much mistaken. The social worker can verify what is true, reject the rest, and work out to their fulfillment the good intentions of these scholars.

Meantime, in order to afford a basis for criticism, and to make a little more concrete the rather vague suggestions so far presented, I shall try to imagine the chapter headings or table of contents of the epoch-making book on character-study which an expert social worker will some day write out of the abundance of his knowledge.

AN OUTLINE STUDY OF CHARACTER

I. THE PHYSIOLOGY OF CHARACTER

(1) *The more or less subconscious seeking of the primal necessities*	Light, air, heat (clothes, shelter), food, water, procreation.

(2) *The Fundamental*   *Their*
    Conscious Tendencies and *Outlets*

(a) Investigation .... { Scientific Interests.
                             Philosophy.

(b) Conquest
    of Nature . { Exploration, subjuga-
                  tion, hunting, ex-
                  ploitation.

    of other men { War, politics, diplo-
                    macy, business,
                    athletics.

(c) Creation, construction, { Art, literature, games,
    play .... government, accumu-
                             lation.

(d) Nurturing .... { Family and friendly
                            relations, nursing,
                            social work, part of
                            medicine, education,
                            care of plants and
                            animals.

(3) *The differentiations and admixtures of these*
    tendencies according to:

(a) Age   { Childhood, adolescence, ma-
                     turity, old age.

(b) Sex

(c) Race   { In this country especially
                     Irish, Jew, and Italian.

(d) Climate and Resi- { City, suburbs, open country,
    dence   seashore, mountains.

(e) Occupation

(f) Economic Status { Rich
                       Poor
                       Comfortable.

(g) Social environment { Family, gang, club,
                          Imitation, Reaction.

(h) Education   i.e., the portion left after
                     excluding the above in-
                     fluences.

II. PATHOLOGY OF CHARACTER

(1) *Exaggerations, deficiencies,* and *perversions* of the tendencies above described (congenital, acquired).

(2) *Paroxysmal and impulsive outbreaks;* temper, tramping, drinking, sexuality.

(3) *Dissociations,* i.e., forgetfulness, tangent-taking, panic-states, cowardice, dissipation.

(4) *Degenerations,* atrophies, formation of fixed, stereotyped habits.

III. CAUSES OF SPECIAL FAULTS

IV. PROGNOSIS

The outlook for various faults, as judged by statistics of cases under standard treatment.

V. TREATMENT

Methods, agencies, laws, institutions, for the prevention, modification, alleviation, or cure of the faults above described.

At present only No. 3c and No. V of this outline are taught to any extent in schools for social workers. Until text-books are gradually built up through systematic research and the statistical study of records, the principle of character-study and character-molding will have to be learned as it has been so far, without books or lectures, but largely:—

(a) By watching the work of experts.

(b) By studying under supervision carefully recorded reports of illustrative

cases.   (The effort to select these would
make of itself a tentative classification or
grouping, which is the beginning of a
science.)

(c) By practicing under careful supervision the actual diagnosis (investigation)
and treatment (disposal) of cases.

I see no reason to doubt that, in the
science and art of character-study and
character-molding, books will ultimately
come to occupy the same useful position
as in medicine, though as educative influences they will always be subordinate (as
they are in medicine) to the watching of
experts at work, the subsequent or pre-
liminary analysis and discussion of printed
cases, and the later apprenticeship in the
work itself.

IV

The need for a clearer recognition of
the new science and center of social work
may be brought out in some other ways.

The organizers of conferences and of schools for social workers find it hard to decide what to include and what to exclude. Programmes contain each year more and more. What shall determine their limits? I should answer, Whatever brings new grist to the mill of character-study and character-molding. Play, for example, is surely an essential element in the expression and formation of children's character. Social workers should study play, playgrounds, and play-apparatus, especially with reference to their value in the development of normal and the prevention of faulty character. Their physical aspect, their economic and municipal aspect is a matter primarily for others.

In a striking and important paper printed about three years ago in *Charities* [1] Lee K. Frankel analyzed the cases of one hundred persons applying to a New York

[1] *Charities,* November 17, 1906.

charitable organization for relief, and studied the causes leading to the application.
He found practically no moral or mental
deficiency, no fault or warping of character. The trouble he concludes is due to
the conditions, the environment in which
these people were forced to live. Apparently then there is nothing here for the
social worker, if I am right in describing
him as a student and physician of character. Do not his figures wholly refute my
thesis?

Let us look again at his figures. In
sixty-two, or practically two-thirds of all
his cases, the destitution was due to illness.
But it was the business of the physician to
have prevented that illness through the
public health authorities, or to have treated
it when it occurred. It is true that physicians do not now prevent or properly treat
such cases; but that does not mean that
the social workers should, except temporarily, take charge of them. Social work-

ers must study the effects of diseases (e.g., malnutrition) upon character, and then do all they can to make the public aware of the harm that is being done, the waste which should be stopped. Social workers must force upon physicians and Health Boards the full weight of their responsibility for the public health.

In the remaining one-third of Mr. Frankel's cases the trouble seemed to be due chiefly to insufficient wages. But social workers cannot do much to raise wages. That is the business of the capitalist and of labor, organized or unorganized. Sickness and low wages it is rarely the social worker's business to cure. *With environment in its effects on character he must constantly deal,* but rarely with the great physical or economic forces that produce the troubles such as Mr. Frankel brings to our notice. I wish especially to emphasize my appreciation of the fact that because the social worker's chief business

is with character, and because his training
should be so shaped as to help him deal
skillfully and appreciatively with character,—for these reasons he must be constantly studying environment. Anyone
who studies character knows how deeply
it is made, molded, or marred by conditions.

But he will study conditions not primarily in their bearing on health, as the
physician should; not on earning power,
which is the business of the captains of
labor, who bend their energies to see how
this environment can be made more pro-
ductive. The social worker should study
the effect of city life, of life on the plains,
of noise, dirt, vice, child-labor, long hours,
not only in their effect on health or income, but especially in their effect on
character. Hygienically it is often imma-
terial whether a room or a person is
clean, but morally it may make a crucial
difference.

Tuberculosis is a matter of great importance both in relation to public health and in relation to the exhaustion of savings with the production of dependency; but it is also and chiefly important to the social worker by reason of the effect which tuberculosis and its treatment may have on the character of the sufferer and of his family. Just here I think the social workers have been somewhat misled by the enthusiasm and vigor of the present public interest in the crusade against tuberculosis. The suppression of tuberculosis is the business of doctors and public health officials. The doctors have been remiss in this matter. It needed the pressure of the general public and of the social workers, spokesmen for the public, to stir the doctors to the proper realization of their duty, but here I think the duty of the social worker should cease. He should not give upon the programmes of his conferences so much space to those aspects of the matter which are primarily the physicians' business.

On the other hand, I hope to see social workers devote more research and energy to the study of how to prevent the doctors from hurting the souls of their tuberculous patients while busy in the attempt to have them live by bread (with milk and eggs) alone. The importance of properly chosen work for the tuberculous patient in different stages of the disease has, I think, been greatly underestimated. The doctor's attention is directed elsewhere. It should be the special business of the social worker to point out that, not for economic but for spiritual reasons, it is a dangerous experiment to take a man away from his work and put him on his back in a steamer-chair for months at a time.

Had the social worker thought of his business not as primarily either physical or financial, nor as that of a worker for the public good in general, but specifically

as that of guarding, building, and developing character, this mistake might have been
more generally recognized and avoided.

Social workers must not labor primarily over the physical aspects of tuberculosis, playgrounds, tenement houses, pris-
ons, garment-workers! Who will watch
over the psychical aspects of every such
bit of social machinery unless the social
worker is awake to this responsibility?
The doctor, the legislator, the economist,
the school teacher, each faces a slightly
different problem. No one but the social
worker is set to watch the spiritual effect
of these agencies. There is danger that
he may not be duly watchful at the post.

The social worker, like the teacher,
should be chiefly an educator, nurturer,
stimulator, developer, and director of human souls, particularly in that group of
persons whose character, temperament, or
environment has brought them into some
sort of trouble.

He is an educator; a school of philanthropy is a normal school; but we must
avoid thinking of the subject-matter in
this sort of normal school as the survey
of the resources, such as almshouses, pris-
ons, playgrounds, probation, etc., which
have already been found useful in his special branch of education. The educator
knows that his subject-matter is never, at
bottom, a subject like geography or history, but always the child's soul, and such
product of other people's souls as may
serve to develop it. For fear of seeming
to lack a sense of humor, the educator can
hardly yet say this to the public, but he
knows that it is true and in " family
gatherings " he admits it. So must the
social worker. There is no more arrogance in the admission for him than for
the teacher. For is it not really true that
the science of social work is not any remedy like relief, or placing out, or almshouses, but primarily the nature and type

of warped, pinched or faulty human souls, and secondarily, the psychical effects of the social remedies which have been worked out experimentally in the past?

The medical student does not begin with the study of drugs, but with anatomy and physiology as aids to diagnosis. He is not primarily concerned with theories of cure. No more should the student of social work be concerned primarily with a bird's-eye view of the existing charitable and reformatory resources of the community, nor with the reforms proposed and laws enacted for the cure of social ills. For this is to learn treatment before diagnosis.

v

It is true enough that you cannot develop a man's character successfully nor appeal effectively to the best that is in him if all the while someone else is sitting on his head. You can't train and strengthen moral fiber if the physical tissues are half starved and the brain deadened by overwork, alcohol, or loss of sleep. Unless the social worker can get someone else to remedy these conditions his work is useless. It is not his business to treat alcoholism or to shut up breweries, to do police work or nurse's work, nor to feed school children. He may be forced in emergencies to pitch into any of these occupations as any citizen will jump into the fire brigade when forest fires threaten a town. But this is not his regular job. He may—nay, he must do all in his power to rouse the properly constituted authorities when child-labor, disease, or lack of employment balks his work. But he cannot be a busybody, a jack of all trades or a " supporter of all good causes " if he is to command respect as an expert in his own field.

If the social worker occupies himself with improving the public schools, the conditions of employment, the law courts, the hospitals, the condition of the streets and tenement houses (as he has recently been advised to do by the editor of *Charities and the Commons*), will he not deserve to be asked whether he has no business of his own to attend to? No man can understand so many subjects.

But he *can* understand a single (for him an all-important) aspect of these intricate subjects; viz., their bearing on character. The doctor cannot know much about electricity;—its effect on human health is the one thing he has time to understand. So the social worker cannot pass judgment on hospital management. But he must be keen to understand (and if possible to neutralize) the harm done to a family when a wife goes to a hospital for some weeks, and thereby deprives her husband and her daughters of the moral support which has hitherto kept them in the straight path.

Shall the social worker effect no radical

reform, no removal of those conditions (poverty, drink, ignorance, disease, overwork, overcrowding) which undermine and vitiate character? Must he confine himself to case work, to palliation, to patching up the broken characters? The answer seems to me this:

If he is wise enough materially to diminish poverty and overwork he is the wisest statesman living and his work should be in statecraft, legislation, and economic reconstruction. There cannot be many such prophets in any century—far too few to constitute a profession. The diminution of ignorance and disease is the work of the educator and the physician through centuries of endeavor,—not a reform to be won at a stroke by anyone.

Every profession must work primarily with individuals—the social worker as well as the rest. Every profession will also try to effect through education, through public opinion, through legislation the removal of the obstacles in the way of its work. Each will call the rest to account when their failures block his path. But none wants to earn the title of walking delegate or professional reformer.

Does not the social worker deal constantly in his work with characters far finer than his own, victims of misfortune and not of their own fault? Surely he does; and he is then the pupil, not the teacher. Social work is still going on, but the positions are reversed.

In other cases there need be no more sense of superiority than the butcher feels when he sells us meat. He has more than we, but he too needs it and eats it himself. So the social worker, like the school teacher, shares with others the knowledge or the enthusiasm by which he himself is guided,—on which he depends. He gives advice, he shares experience, he helps to make plans simply because he has been in such scrapes before, not because

he arrogates any especial merit to
himself.

VI

Once thoroughly equipped and recognized as an expert in the understanding
and management of the weaknesses and
perversions of character, the social worker
should command expert fees.   He should
have his office hours and his private practice as well as his public work among the
poor.   He should be consulted as Mark
Fagan used to be consulted, as Professor
Royce is often consulted, by rich and poor,
in all sorts of moral and domestic difficulties, by the parents of difficult children,
by the children of difficult parents, and
also by many neurasthenics seen in consultation with physicians.   The average
social worker is, in my opinion, far better
equipped to treat neurasthenia than the
average physician is.   The mental and
moral aspects of such cases altogether

overshadow their physical aspects, and the problems of occupation, of encouragement, of foresight, hindsight, and of responsible living are just what the social worker is constantly encountering.

I see no reason why social work should be done chiefly among the poor. My most intimate and thorough knowledge of the topic has been gained through the social work done by my wife on me. Social work (the understanding and molding of faulty character) is possible, I know, because I have experienced it in the hands of an expert.

CHAPTER III

DESPITE the distinctions emphasized in the last chapter, history shows that medical work and social work are branches split off from a common trunk:—*the care of people in trouble.* In earlier centuries the priest healed the sick, cared for the poor, taught the ignorant, and often led his people in industrial, governmental, and even in martial activities. He was the lawgiver and magistrate, the doctor, the school-teacher, the dispenser of charity, the temporal ruler, and sometimes the leader in war. Such all-inclusive usefulness in the priesthood still lingers here and

there among us. Father Nisco in the little
town of Roseto, Penn. (see *McClure's
Magazine,* January, 1908), is doing something very like this now. He is the leader
of his town in industrial, municipal, and
political life as well as in educational and
spiritual affairs.

In a similar way, the country doctor,
the old-fashioned family physician, has
sometimes extended his profession as
widely and deeply as the priest was once
allowed to do. Barrie and Watson have
described such doctors and many of us
have known them, leaders in all civic work.

But specialization of work and division
of labor have come into the field once occu-
pied alone by the minister or the doctor.
The doctor is now supposed to care for the
diseased body, the teacher for the undeveloped mind, the minister for the needy
soul, the social worker for the poor, while
justice and governmental work are like-
wise intrusted to specialists. On the

whole, doubtless, this division of labor is good for every resulting profession except that of the minister, but what I wish here to point out is that in this field, as in many others, *division of labor is never an unmixed blessing* and may easily become a curse unless energy and intelligence are devoted to the ways and means of attaining a close co-operation and interchange of ideas, methods, and plans among the divided laborers.

There is a distinction and an important one between the troubles of mind, of body, and of estate; but there is also a unity among them. Hence no one can give the most efficient aid to a diseased body, a distracted or undeveloped mind, or a needy family without crossing the dividing lines and laboring in fields assigned primarily to others. A doctor needs to know something of social work and of the spiritual and mental life of his patients. A social worker must know something of physiology and hygiene, and all educators, whether lay or clerical, must know something both of medicine and of social work.

I recently saw a priest create a strong, but most unfavorable, impression at the graduation exercises of a training school for nurses when he said, addressing the doctors and nurses present: " *You* deal with the body, *I* with the soul." Our practice has gone far beyond this academic theory. Despite Professor Münsterberg's plea for armed neutrality [1] no such sharp boundaries can be maintained. The ancient controversy between materialism and spiritualism is ended. There are no crass materialists or rampant spiritualists among the working professions. Matter and spirit belong together; neither of them independent, neither slavishly subordinate. Each interpenetrates everywhere and whosoever neglects either in his field of work comes to grief.

[1] "Psychotherapy ": New York, 1909.

Among my friends I am proud to number two cousins who are members of the famous Worcester family, Elwood Worcester of Boston and Alfred Worcester of Waltham. Both are doctors, the first a doctor of divinity, the second a doctor of medicine, but Elwood Worcester, the minister of religion, is now known and blessed all over the country as a healer of souls (and incidentally of bodies) through his psychotherapeutic work at Emmanuel Church; while Alfred Worcester, the doctor, is even more famous as a trainer of souls than as a healer of bodies. Each is distinguished within his own narrower field; each is still more distinguished for his success in work that overlaps and goes far to erase the faint lines of division between his own profession and that of his cousin.

Why is this so?

Simply because wherever troubles are heaped up and gathered together as they are in a hospital, in a mission church, in the offices of a relief society, we find that those troubles are *assorted*. They are not neatly separated, each in its own corner. They do not heed our academic distinctions or our divisions of labor. Poverty, disease, moral shiftlessness, and spiritual torment are inextricably intermingled in the face and fortunes of a single sufferer. Not even the sufferer himself can tell what is root and what is branch among his troubles. He will wander into a hospital in search of a tonic (" something to give me strength, doctor "), although his weakness may be due to lack of food and that lack to the loss of his job. He will run to a clergyman distracted with religious doubts when the root of his troubles is insomnia. In all such cases *he goes to the wrong shop* and the shopman (doctor, minister, social worker) is apt to take him at his own valuation, to treat him for his stomach if he complains of that or for his

atheism if that is the burden of his re-
marks. Disaster often results.

Let me exemplify more in detail the extraordinary intermingling of the afflictions
of mind, body, and estate as we meet them
in all sorts and conditions of men.

I

Mental or spiritual turmoil for physical
reasons

(a) *Religious ecstasies, moral doubts,*
and *self-condemnations* are often manifestations of insanity, of hysteria, of neurasthenia, or of the stresses of adolescence
with its torrential flood of developing energies. Suffering of this kind often leads
people to seek help from a clergyman.
But unless the clergyman is on his guard
he will make a bad matter worse. The in-
tense " conviction of sin," which such a
sufferer often experiences, may be as morbid as the dreams of an opium eater, something that vanishes and ought to vanish

with the return of health. The religious
ecstasies and visions which the evangelist
might welcome and encourage in his young
pupil may yet possess no more spiritual
significance than the black cats and snakes
at which the alcoholic snatches in his de-
lirium. I am far from asserting that all
religious visions are morbid. I am merely
recalling the well-known fact that *some*
religious visions are morbid, and that unless clergymen work in close touch with
medical men and medical ideas they may
do unnecessary harm by encouraging the
wrong vision.

(b) *Excessive worry, timidity, scrupu-
losity* is often an early symptom (though
mistaken for the cause) of arteriosclerosis,
of Bright's disease, anæmia, or tuberculosis. " Poor man! " (people say.)
" Business worry, too heavy responsibil-
ities, too long hours of work broke him
down." Doubtless this is sometimes a
true bill, but irregular meals, frequent nips

of whiskey, and advancing arterial degeneration are often more potent than the psychical causes. A child's fear of the dark may vanish after a summer in the open air and return again after a winter's " education " in stuffy schoolrooms and cramped positions. In this sense it is " physical " in origin.

(c) *Laziness, shiftlessness, carelessness,* may be only the mental manifestations of the debility of adolescence, of chorea, of cerebral disease, of malnutrition, or of any of the other diseases mentioned above. I once heard a social worker illustrating out of her own bitter experience the need of more medical knowledge or medical co-operation for the members of her profession: " He seemed to be getting lazier and lazier, every motion slower and slower. It took him an interminable while to get dressed and out at work in the morning. He lost place after place. We tried first to appeal to his ambition, then to his affection for his wife and children. We tried encouragement and reproof. We got the priest to use his influence. There was some improvement. The man evidently tried hard for a time, but he seemed to get no satisfaction out of his dawning prosperity. His spirits sank lower and lower, till he was so depressed that an alienist was consulted. Insanity was the expert's verdict; and all that I had interpreted as moral slackness was undoubtedly, he said, the ' psycho-motor retardation' characteristic of an early stage of depressive-manic insanity. He is in an asylum still. I wish I hadn't plagued him so for what wasn't his fault."

But though I am keenly aware of the dangers of mistakes due to overlooking the physical conditions just alluded to, I think that we all of us, doctors, teachers, ministers, social workers, need to be just as alert to avoid the opposite error.

II

Physical complaints and even diseases may be due to mental and spiritual causes, to ignorance, mental disease, and sin

(a) The fear-neuroses, the habit-pains, the hysterical paralyses, spasms, and anæsthesias are among the more common and obvious examples, often wrongly treated by drugs and physical means alone.

(b) Many people are sick because of remorse more or less stifled, because of animosities or slights brooded over, because of loss or disappointment to which they do not become reconciled.

(c) Ignorance of the laws of health, of the workings of the organs of nutrition and reproduction, of the influence of mind on body and of body on mind is certainly a prolific cause of disease.

III

*Financial dependence and want is more
and more often seen to be the result of
physical and mental causes. People are
poor because they are sick and ignorant*

In illustration of this I need only remind you of the great prevalence of tuberculosis, typhoid, and other infectious diseases among the poor, and of the facts
cited by Lee K. Frankel, in the article to
which I have already referred (see page
76). In 62 out of 100 successive cases
applying to a relief agency the destitution
of the applicant was due to illness.

Old age, accident, alcoholism, acute and
chronic disease, the death of the bread win-
ner, are among the commonest causes of
financial distress in America. Hence the
social worker must be in the closest touch
with physicians and must, in my opinion,
know a good deal of medicine, as, in fact,
he often does.

In the last chapter I tried to show how far character-defects are responsible for many of the problems with which social workers are concerned. Here I will not repeat what was then said. That the diagnosis and treatment of character in difficulties is the business of social workers who deal with children, with delinquents and the whole field of probation work is, I think, obvious. It is not quite so obvious that behind the effort to remove any of the causes of financial troubles or poverty is an *educational* problem. We ought to educate *somebody* every time we receive an application for financial relief. It may be the applicant himself whose ignorance, forgetfulness, lack of imagination or of concentration are responsible for his failure. More often it is the duty of the social worker to begin an educational crusade against the ignorance of those who are responsible for the bad conditions which produced the bankruptcy. Someone in the community surely needs education. It may be the employer who permits unsanitary work-conditions, though they may hurt his own pocket as well as the health of his employees. It may be the legislators whose error of omission or of commission are responsible for health-killing conditions in factories, schools, tenements, and railroads. It may be the bargain hunters and the fashion slaves, whose shortsightedness makes starvation wages and irregular employment so common.

But however difficult it may be to catch the man who needs education, we may be sure that he is there and we must make an intelligent effort to find and to " reach " him, so fatally dependent are mind, body, and estate; the mind of one and the body and estate of others, in this field.

So far I have spoken of:

1. The dependence of mental on bodily trouble.

2. The dependence of bodily on mental trouble.

3. The dependence of financial on bodily and mental trouble.

Naturally enough the interdependencies which I have been pointing out are tending to bring together again the doctor and the social worker, whose now divided functions were once united, and to emphasize for them both the importance of education in the remedy of all mental, physical, and financial troubles. What I have said may be thus summed up:

Doctor and social worker must each look to the other for the causes of the trouble he seeks to cure. At bottom medical ills are largely social, and social ills largely medical. *But both doctor and social worker, when they have learned (each from the other) the deeper causes of their patients' ills, must go hand in hand to the educator, or at any rate must betake themselves to educational methods, when they get through with diagnosis and begin treatment.*

The dependence of doctor and social worker on education and on the educator has been made so clear by the success of educational campaigns against tuberculosis, alcoholism, child labor, dark tenements, and unprotected machinery that I do not care to dwell on it here. I wish rather to point out the reverse, namely:

The dependence of the educator on the doctor and on the social worker.

The educator and those in charge of education are becoming increasingly aware of the fact that since a compulsory school law forces the children to undergo many dangers (as well as to receive many benefits), justice and common sense say: "Neutralize so far as possible the peculiar dangers of school life." Such dangers are:—

1. Those resulting from keeping your

children indoors and making them sit still
and use small muscles (eye and hand).

2. Those resulting from eyestrain.

3. Those resulting from acute infectious
diseases and from tuberculosis.

4. Those resulting from discouragement, ostracism, and handicapping of
the child by adenoids or speech defect, ac-
centuated by school work and school discipline.

To neutralize, prevent, or minimize
these evils, the school authorities are beginning to institute:

(a) Physical as well as mental exam-
inations (especially in New York and Boston).

(b) Psycho-physical tests (especially
in Chicago and Philadelphia).

(c) School nurses.

(d) Physical training, school-gardens,
and proper playgrounds.

Since the causes of many of the ills
which doctors, educators, and social work-

ers are combating lie across the boundaries that separate these professions from each other, the realization of this fact plus the desire to be thorough, to leave no stone unturned in searching out causes, is changing all three professions.

I

Changes in the Medical Profession

Doctors are realizing that they must know more than they do of

(a) *Diagnostic psychology*: i.e., the scientific study of character in health and in disease.

(b) *Therapeutic psychology*: the systematic application of mental methods to the cure of disease.

(c) *Educational psychology*: the science and art of pedagogy as applied to the training of sick minds, sick wills, and ungoverned emotions.

(d) *Social work*: the bearing of industrial, domestic, and economic conditions on health.

(e) The possibilities of moral, and thereby of physical, harm resulting from some current methods of treating patients; i.e., the undermining of character and the disintegration of families through the idleness and isolation forced on phthisical patients; the drug-habits and doctor-habits produced by the giving of placebos and the telling of soothing lies.

(f) *Preventive medicine:* (see below).

II

Changes in the Profession of Social Work

(a) Social workers are learning and applying more of the doctor's stock-in-trade, physiology, hygiene, and mental healing.

(b) They are at present taking the lead in *preventive medicine,* i.e., in the improvement of milk supplies, tenements and parks, in the crusade against tuberculosis and alcoholism, in the organization of public sentiment leading to legislation for the introduction of school nurses, the medical examination of school children, the passage of child labor laws, pure food and drug laws, the medical inspection of factories, dairies, bakeries, and packing houses.

(c) Social workers are finding their place in hospitals, factories, and churches where the social problems may overshadow the industrial, surgical, or technically religious work.

(d) Such problems as that of blindness, formerly attacked merely from the medical side, are now being treated from the educational and industrial standpoint by social workers.

III

Changes in the profession of teaching both clerical and secular

(a) Clergymen and other teachers are resuming their ancient functions of ministering to sick souls, i.e., the neurasthenics, hysterics, and those burdened by unreasoning fears, vicious habits, and distracting thoughts.

(b) Lay teachers are beginning to apply to their teaching some rudimentary knowledge of physiology, of hygiene, of psychology, and of social work.

(c) Hygiene and social ethics are beginning to be taught in school.

(d) Schools are beginning to be used as social centers, for evening recreation classes, clubs, and lectures.

(e) Colleges are providing free public lectures on medical topics and are beginning to take more responsibility for the student's whole character and not merely for his intellectual development.[1]

One Result of These Changes

No one can have followed the history of the last ten years in medicine, education,

[1] Woodrow Wilson: Address to the Phi Beta Kappa Society at Harvard, July 1st, 1909, and A. Lawrence

and social work and noted the increasing evidence of their interpenetration and closer co-operation without discerning:

(a) The rapid growth of public medicine, whose method is educational, preventive, and sociological;

(b) The consequent restriction of the sphere of the " private doctor."

With the increasing power and respect commanded by municipal, state, and national health boards it becomes possible for such boards to open and manage a municipal milk-depot with teacher nurses, as in Rochester, N. Y.; to enforce the anti-spitting laws as in parts of New York City; to investigate and control bakeries, dairies, packing houses, and water supplies. Even Philadelphia has finally (1909) ceased to endure public murder (through typhoid germs) at the hands of its city government.

Lowell: Competition in College, *Atlantic Monthly,* June, 1909.

National medicine made a start in 1900 when it unmasked the lies and trickery by which the San Francisco city government concealed the existence of bubonic plague in that city. It advanced a long step in 1904 when Colonel Gorgas was promoted from a subordinate medical officer to a full member of the Panama Canal Commission and given power to stamp out yellow fever and to curb malaria on the Isthmus. It advanced two long steps in 1907 when the Meat Inspection bill brought the packers to their senses, and the Pure Food and Drug bill broke the power of the Patent Medicines.

School hygiene has now become the most important branch of public medicine, for in the school population the state can influence the health of all its future citizens, putting its guiding hand upon them at the most critical period in their lives. School nurses, medical inspection, and systematic treatment of school children, school playgrounds under the control and management of the school itself (as by the Massachusetts law of 1907); the teaching of hygiene, mental and physical, in schools and colleges, all mark a long step in the advance of public, preventive, educational medicine.

This, together with the development of factory inspection, protection of machinery, tenement house legislation, public parks, baths and playgrounds, the growing efficiency of public diagnosis-laboratories and free drugs (quinine, diphtheria anti-toxin, and in Porto Rico thymol), is driving the private doctor more and more to the wall. The " good, old-fashioned " epidemics of typhoid, diphtheria, and malaria are getting rarer and the doctors are feeling the loss of income. Yellow fever and smallpox are gone. The number of chronic invalids requiring long and expensive medical attendance is being diminished by the growth of successful surgery,

of efficient psychotherapeutics, of outdoor
life, and by the sanatorium treatment of
tuberculosis.

Partly as a result of this, the number of
doctors and of medical students has begun
within the past five years to diminish not
only in America but in all parts of Eu-
rope. We doctors are actually beginning
to abolish ourselves by merging ourselves
in the wider profession of public, preventive medicine, whose activities are inextricably interwoven, as this chapter aims to
show, with social and educational work. I
am thankful that it is so.

Here are the cheerful facts: [1]

	1905	1908
Medical students	25,835	22,787
Population of U. S. (estimated)	83,143,000	87,170,000
Ratio of students to population	1 : 3,218	1 : 3,825

[1] See Report of U. S. Commissioner of Education.
Vol. II, p. 777, 1908.

CHAPTER IV

TEAM-WORK OF DOCTOR AND PATIENT
THROUGH THE ANNIHILATION
OF LYING

TEAM-WORK, genuine co-operation, has
been my guiding interest throughout this
book. It is largely because people can't
or won't pull together that the world
moves on no faster than it does. We are
held apart by professional narrowness and
professional case-hardening (as when a
nurse refuses to help a gasping, broken-
winded teamster up the hospital stairs,
"because it is the ward tender's business"), or by mutual suspicion (as between ministers and doctors), or simply
by ignorance of each other's existence.
But still more I think we hold each other
at arm's length by our persistent habits

of lying and prevarication. A doctor lies to his patient about the medicine which he is asked to take. The patient pours the medicine down the sink and lies to the doctor about it. Poor team-work, that! Friends cool down to mere acquaintance-ship because their cordial faces and effu-sive manners don't prevent their reading behind the mask (with the marvelous in-sight of aroused suspicion) what each has said of each in other company.

I believe that the art of healing is going to spring ahead with astonishing swiftness in the next decade because the community is coming to realize that doctor and patient can work together to exterminate or limit disease. Preventive medicine, first fos-tered by the social workers and by the national government, now tardily taken up by the medical profession in great cities, makes for frankness, for education of the whole public, for the general diffusion of medical knowledge, and for the abolition of professional secrecy and unprofessional buncombe.

But the battle is still not won. Far from it! The great bulk of medical work, public and private, is still done by men—high-minded men—who believe that it is impossible to deal frankly and openly with patients. The social workers are not always as truthful as they might be. The head of a great humanitarian enterprise recently asked me to co-operate with her in a complicated deception of one of her temporary employees. When I remonstrated with her, she quoted to me Lecky's saying that in such matters we must be guided by " a combination of good sense and good feeling." Her good sense and good feeling taught her to lie in the same kindly paternal way used by many doctors when they fool their patients, strictly for the latter's good, but still to the destruction of all team-work and enlightenment.

I have thought it worth while, therefore,

to report as objectively as I can my own experience with lying and with veracity in medicine.

I approach the subject of truth in medicine, not from the point of view of scientific method, nor of metaphysical analysis, but of professional ethics. I do not ask " how can we find truth," nor " what is truth," but " how far should we speak the truth in dealing with our patients, our colleagues, or anyone else? " " Are lies ever in place? If so, under what conditions? "

My method is experimental, the only one in which reasonable men place confidence, the only sound, scientific method. I shall not discuss the general principles, the authorities, or traditions which might guide our course in this matter. As indicated in the title of this chapter I have made an experimental study of two different hypotheses on the subject, submitting them to the test of experience, as any candid person must, if he wishes to make the fairest judgment in his power on any question. I have been working on this subject during a considerable part of the last eighteen years, and my conclusions, however faulty they may be, must be criticised like any other piece of scientific work only by those who have repeated the experiments on which they are based.

I began, as was natural, with the hypothesis on which I had been brought up. My medical training included some few lectures on medical ethics, but in such matters example far more than precept was the guide of the Harvard medical student of my day. Only once during my course was the question of veracity in medical matters directly treated.

" When you are thinking of telling a lie," said the teacher, " ask yourself whether it is simply and solely for the patient's benefit that you are going to tell it. If you are sure that you are acting for his good and not for your own profit, you can go ahead with a clear conscience."

The lies which the medical profession agree in condemning are those told for personal and private gain. The magazine article representing work never performed and written solely for advertising purposes, is a lie that no one approves. The diagnosis of diphtheria when the physician knows the case is merely one of tonsilitis, is not justified by the increased fees which his frequent visits entail. There is no disagreement of opinion among physicians about such lies as these.

But the lies which are usually defended among physicians are of a different type and may be illustrated by the following quotations:

" The young physician in our day has some advantages in competition with older men. People sometimes consider a young man more up-to-date than his elders. Still there are some alleviations in growing old.

When you don't know what's the matter with a patient you can then enjoy the luxury of saying so. When you're young you have to know everything, for if you say you don't know, the patient is likely to chuck you out and send for someone else, who does."

That veracity in diagnosis is possible for the older physician, but not always for the younger, seems to be the moral of this quotation.

Veracity in prognosis is even harder. In the course of a lecture on the prognosis of heart disease, I once heard the following story:

A business man past middle life was found to be suffering from some form of heart disease. His wife inquired about the diagnosis and hearing it was heart disease, she asked: " Isn't it true that he may drop dead suddenly? " The doctor had to confess that this was a possibility. " The consequence was," went on the story-teller,

" that day after day she sat at her window about the time that her husband should be returning from business, watching to see whether he would come home on his feet or in an ambulance."

" Now," said the narrator, " when you get into practice, gentlemen, whatever you do, don't do that. Don't make a woman's life miserable because you can't keep a fact to yourself."

Surely it seems as if this is the place for a good straight lie. I thought so when I heard the story and made up my mind that, whatever blunders I made in dealing with any patients I might have, this one I would avoid. But I found it more difficult than I had anticipated. It was not very many years before I saw in consultation a case the duplicate of that just described. Mr. B. had angina pectoris, with serious disease of his heart and kidneys. He needed rest. He had refused to take it, and the chances were that he would continue to force himself along until he dropped in his tracks. After I had talked over the case with the attending physician and was about to return and say a word to the family, my colleague said: " There's one thing I must warn you about. This man's wife is an excessively nervous, excitable woman of no stamina at all. She gets hysterical on the slightest pretext, and when that happens she makes everyone else in the house sick. If she hears what's the matter with her husband, she'll go all to pieces. So you'll be very guarded in what you say, won't you? " To this I readily agreed. Remembering my lesson, we went downstairs where Mrs. B. was waiting to hear the result of our deliberations. She placed a chair for me and then planted herself in another, squarely facing me and very near. " Now, first of all," said she, " I want to know whether you are going to give me a straight and true answer to everything I ask you? " Having just promised the family physician that I would do nothing of the kind, I was so taken aback that I hesitated a moment. "That's enough," said Mrs. B., getting up. "I don't care to hear anything more from you."

I did not blame her. She had fairly caught us in our attempt to trick her. But the anecdote shows that the path of the medical man who conscientiously tries to shield people from pain and trouble is sometimes a difficult and thorny one.

By means of these examples I hope I have succeeded in making clear the problems that I wish next to discuss more in detail.

I propose now to consider: (1) Veracity in diagnosis; (2) Veracity in prognosis; (3) Veracity in treatment.

By veracity I mean doing one's best to convey to another person the impression that one has about the matter in hand.

One may do one's best and yet fail; but that is not lying. I once spent half an hour trying to convey to my parlor girl my impression about how to build a wood fire, but when she next tried to build one it appeared that the only idea she had received was that of packing kindling wood into the fireplace as tightly as she could and piling logs on top, without leaving a chink or cranny anywhere for a draft. Clearly I did not succeed in conveying my impression to her, yet I suppose no one will accuse me of lying to her.

A true impression, not certain words literally true, is what we must try to convey. When a patient who has the earliest recognizable signs of phthisis in one lung, and tubercle bacilli in his sputum, asks, " Have I got consumption? " it would be conveying a false impression to say, " Yes, you have," and stop there. Ten to one his impression is that by consumption I mean a disease invariably and rapidly fatal.

But this is not at all my impression of his case. To be true to that patient one must explain that what *he* means by consumption is the later stages of a neglected or unrecognized disease; that some people have as much trouble as he now has and get over it without finding it out; that with climatic and hygienic treatment he has a good chance of recovery, etc. To tell him simply that he has consumption without adding any further explanation would convey an impression which in one sense is true, in the sense, namely, that to another physician it might sound approximately correct. What is sometimes called the simple truth, the " bald truth," or the " naked truth," is often practically false— as unrecognizable as Lear naked upon the moor. It needs to be explained, supplemented, modified.

Bearing in mind, then, that by veracity I mean the faithful attempt to convey a true impression, and by lying an *inten-*

tional deception, however brought about;
let us take up the question of

I

Truth and Falsehood in Diagnosis

The common conception of a doctor's
duty in this matter, and one according to
which I practiced medicine for the first
five or six years after my graduation, is
something as follows:

" Tell the truth so far as possible. But
if you are young and not yet firmly established in practice, it won't do to let the patient or his family know when you are in
doubt about a diagnosis. If you do, they
will lose confidence in you and perhaps
turn you out."

That is what is implied in the frank and
refreshing confession of a middle-aged
and successful physician whose words I
have already quoted: " The great advantage of getting old is that when you

don't know, you can enjoy the luxury of saying so."

The first experience that made me doubt whether it was necessary for a young practitioner to pretend omniscience in order to retain his patients' confidence was the following: I had the opportunity of driving about a large town some twenty-five miles from Boston with a young physician only a year or two my senior. He took me on his regular rounds; we saw farmers and the grocer's wife, the hotel-keeper's daughter, and the blacksmith's baby, as well as one or two well-to-do people. The great majority of the cases were in families of very limited education, the kind of folks that we think of as subsisting mostly on pies and patent medicine. But what made each case an eye-opener to me was the utter frankness of the doctor with the families. Diagnosis, prognosis, and treatment were given with an absence of subterfuge and of prevarication that astounded

me, and what surprised me even more was
to see the way the patients liked his frankness. I never have seen manifested more
implicit confidence in a physician than
during that drive. He never forced his
doubts or his suspicions upon his patients,
but when they asked a straight question
they got a straight answer. A baby had a
fever. " What's the baby got? " asked its
mother. " Can't tell yet," said the doctor;
" may be going to break out with something to-morrow, or it may be all right in
a day or two. We shall have to wait and
see." There was no talk of " febricula "
or " gastric fever." Not once did I hear
him say that a patient was " *threatened* "
with any disease. He knew that Nature
makes no threats and that no honest doctor
ever foists his ignorance upon " Nature "
by charging her with making a " threat."

I asked him the obvious question:
" How can you be so frank with your
patients and yet keep their confidence? "

"Because they know," said he, "that whenever anything unusual comes up that I can't handle or that puzzles me I have a consultant. So when I say that I do know, they believe me, and when I say I don't know and yet don't call in a consultant they understand that nothing of any seriousness is the matter, and that they don't need to worry. Lots of men are afraid to call a consultant because they are afraid the family will think the less of their ability. But it makes the family feel a great deal safer to know that I don't pretend to know everything and stand ready any moment to call in someone who knows more than I do. I've seen a man lose a family because he *didn't* have a consultant, but never because he did."

"Don't the families ever object to the expense of a consultant?" I asked.

"No," said he, "it's perfectly easy to get good consultants at low prices if you explain the family's circumstances to them."

As a result of that conversation I began cautiously to try the experiment of telling the truth, whether I understood the case thoroughly or not. I never had reason to regret it, and I am every year more firmly convinced that the young doctor, even when practicing chiefly among uneducated people, does not need to pretend omniscience merely because he is young and his patients ignorant. The truth works just as well for the pocket, and a great deal better for the community and for our own self-respect.

" A certain profession of dogmatism," said Sir Frederick Treves in an address [1] to medical students, " is essential in the treatment of the sick. The sick man will allow of no hesitancy in the recognition of disease. He blindly demands that the appearance of knowledge shall be absolute,

[1] *British Medical Journal,* October 18, 1902.

however shadowy and unsubstantial may be the bases of it."

This declaration has the great merit of frankness. But how would a doctor like to have his patients hear those words? How would he like to be caught by his patients in the act of passing on to medical students such little tricks of the trade as this? It is true that his address may never come to his patients' ears; he may never be found out. But is it good for us as professional men to have our reputations rest on the expectation of not being found out?

I doubt beside whether (as Dr. Gould [1] once pointed out in an admirable editorial) we " succeed in humbugging the patient's relations and friends by the devices which apparently suit the patient. Among intelligent laymen, far more frequently than is supposed, one finds that such sham certainty without the reality of knowledge

[1] American Medicine, November 1, 1902, p. 681.

and conviction is at once detected. Doctors make a great mistake when they think their deceits really deceive.

Then there is the patient who recovers. When he is well, the false diagnoses, the changes of dogmatic opinions and of medicines, the blind alley of proved errors, these are thought over."

It is getting steadily harder to deceive the public. Some years ago I heard a prominent and representative citizen of Boston commenting upon the medical bulletins on ex-President Roosevelt's leg. " Of course," he said, " no one ever believes these bulletins. The doctors give out only so much as they think fit, in order not to alarm the public unnecessarily. The result is that the public never believes the bulletins and is always more or less anxious."

Now, I do not believe that the truth was in any way tampered with in the bulletins either of President Roosevelt's or of

President McKinley's illness. I believe
these bulletins gave the strict and accurate
truth. But I think it is generally admitted
that such bulletins do not command the
respect which they usually deserve. Business men and others to whom it may be of
vital importance to get reliable information about the illness, are especially apt to
" discount " the bulletins of the group of
physicians in attendance on a man whose
life is of great importance financially. We
all remember how persistently the general
public believed that King Edward's illness
of 1902 was due to malignant disease, and
not to the " perityphlitis " mentioned in
the bulletins. How can we blame the public for not believing the doctors in attendance on the King when one of them, Sir
Frederick Treves, is willing publicly to
advocate the systematic deception of patients? His words I have quoted. It is
true that he does not advise deception
under conditions like those of King Ed-

ward's illness, but how is the public to know just when and how far the doctor will think it best to deceive? Such discrimination is especially difficult in a country like England, where the public cannot help knowing that what is " given out " concerning foreign affairs, especially in matters of diplomacy and war, represents only so much of the truth as the officials think it best for the public to know.

I have been speaking of the disadvantages of trying to deceive a patient or those interested in him with regard to the diagnosis. I have argued so far that it is not necessary to assume absolute knowledge in order to impress the patient's mind and hold his confidence, and that owing to the increasing scepticism of the public, it is becoming more and more difficult to fool the patient at all.

Very few Americans like to lie. They would rather tell the truth if they could, but there are cases in which the voice of duty itself seems to tell us that we must lie. To prevent the breaking up of a family, to save a life, are we not to lie? A husband confesses to you the sin that has resulted in disease for him. The wife, suspecting something, catches you on your way out and asks you point-blank what ails her husband. Can you tell her the truth? Well, suppose you tell her a good, round, well-constructed lie. What are the chances of her believing you? If she has got to the point of suspecting her husband, are her suspicions likely to be quieted permanently by your reassurances? Is there not a fair chance that she knows enough of the usual customs of physicians when placed in this position, to discount what you say?

The truth in such matters very often comes to light sooner or later, and if it does, the wife is apt to let a number of persons know what kind of a trick you have played her. Of course, there are many such cases in which the truth is never found out, but I ask again, is it a good thing for us as professional men to be living in the hope of not being found out?

II

Truth and Falsehood in Prognosis

That it is a bad thing to lie about a prognosis we all admit, as a general rule, but there are cases when it is not easy to see what harm it does when the good that it does is very evident indeed.

A patient has gastric cancer. He is told that he has neuralgia of the stomach, and feels greatly relieved by the reassurance, for the effect of psychic influences is nowhere more striking than in gastric cancer (as the cases quoted in Osler's textbook show). Meantime the truth is told to the patient's wife, and she makes whatever preparations are necessary for the inevitable end. Now what harm can be done

by such a lie as this? The sufferer is pro-
tected from anticipations and forebodings
which are often the worst portion of his
misery, while his wife, knowing the truth
and thoroughly approving of the deception, is able to see that her husband's financial affairs are straightened out and
to prepare, as well as may be, for his
death. Surely this seems a humane and
sensible way to ease the patient's hard
path, and who can be the worse off
for it?

I answer, " Many may be worse off for
it, and some must be." The patient himself
is very possibly saved some suffering.
But consider a minute. His wife has now
acquired, if she did not have it already, a
knowledge of the circumstances under
which doctors think it merciful and useful
to lie. She will be sick herself some day,
and when the doctors tell her that she is
not seriously ill, is she likely to believe
them?

I was talking on this subject not long ago with a girl of twenty-two. " Oh, of course, I never believe what doctors say," was her comment, " for I've helped 'em lie too often and helped fix up the letters that were written so that no one should suspect the truth."

In other words such lies simply transfer to the future account of one person, the sufferings which we spare another. We rob Peter to pay Paul.

But it is not likely that the mischief will be so closely limited. There are almost always other members of the family who are let into the secret; servants, nurses, and intimate friends, either before or after the patient's death, find out what is going on. All told, I doubt if there are less than a dozen souls on the average who are enlightened by such a case in regard to the standards of the physician in charge and so of the profession he represents. I have heard such things talked over among " the laity," and, as a rule, not one, but several cases are adduced to exemplify the prevailing customs of medical men in such circumstances.

We think we can isolate a lie as we do a case of smallpox, and let its effect die with the occasion that brought it about. But is it not common experience that such customs are infectious and spread far beyond our intention and our control? They beget, as a rule, not any acute indignation among those who get wind of them (for " how," they say, " could the doctor do otherwise "), but rather a quiet, chronic incredulity which is stubborn just in proportion as it is vitally important in a given case to get at the truth, as in the case of King Edward before mentioned.

You will notice that I am not now arguing that a lie is, in itself and apart from its consequences, a bad thing. I am not saying that we ought to tell the truth in order to save our own souls or keep ourselves untainted. I am saying that many a lie saves present pain at the expense of greater future pain, and that if we saw as clearly the future harm as we see the present good, we could not help seeing that the balance is on the side of harm. Only intellectual short-sightedness blinds us to this.

I have told fully my share of lies, under the impression, shared, I think, by many of the profession, that it is necessary in exceptional cases to do it for the good of the patient and his friends; but since I have been experimenting with the policy of telling the truth (at first cautiously, but lately with more confidence), I have become convinced that the necessity is a specious one, that the truth works better for all concerned, not only in the long run, but in relatively short spurts, and that its good results are not postponed to eternity, but are usually discernible within a short time.

In vindication of my belief let me relate the sequel to one of the stories already told. The reader will recall that I prepared " to be very guarded in what I said " (as the technical phrase is) to a lady whose husband had angina pectoris. The attending physician, who had known the lady for years, and who represented entirely the views of her family, assured me that she was too delicate and too unstrung by neurasthenia to be capable of bearing the truth about her husband. If she knew that he might at any time die suddenly, she would brood and fret over the knowledge until she became so querulous and unhinged that all the family, the sick husband included, would be made miserable. It will be remembered that I made up my mind to conceal the truth from her if I could, and how she upset all my calculations by asking me suddenly whether or not I would tell her the whole truth so far as I knew it.

Now consider a moment the difficulties of that situation.

" Will you give me a true answer to every question I ask you?" I could scarcely be expected to pop out a prompt " yes " when I had just promised the family physician not to do anything of the sort. Of course I could not say " no," and if I hesitated an instant, I had betrayed my intention of deceiving her. What would you have done?

As a matter of fact I hesitated a bit, as I think anyone but a most practiced liar or a hide-bound truth-teller would have done. " That's enough," said she; " that's all I want to hear." But of course I couldn't leave it there, so I pulled myself together and made a clean breast of the whole thing. I told her just what I thought and what I expected, including all that I had promised the doctor not to tell. Now you will remember that the attending physician, who had known her intimately for years, had warned me that she could not bear this sort of news— that she would brood and worry over it, until she had made herself and everyone else in the house miserable. So when she cornered me and got the truth out of me, I made haste to get out of the house, and thanked my stars that I did not have to stay behind and pick up the pieces of the nervous wreck to which my plain, unvarnished tale must needs reduce the poor lady.

Several weeks after, I met the family physician and learned that for some mysterious reason the expected collapse on the part of the neurotic wife had never arrived. Everyone was still expecting her to go to pieces, but as yet she had got along about as usual. In point of fact she has never met their expectation. It is now nearly fourteen years since the dreadful truth was told her and no breakdown has occurred.

After that most astonishing experience
I began cautiously to tell the truth in
similar cases, even though intimate friends
or relations of the patient declared that
the truth could not be borne, and even
when I had no knowledge of the patient's
character to set against that of his closest
friends.   It has been, on the whole, the
most interesting and surprising experiment that I have ever tried.   The astound-
ing *innocuousness of the truth* when all
reason and all experience would lead one
to believe it must do harm, has never
ceased to surprise me.   It seems as if when
the pinch comes and the individual has to
face stern realities, some species of anti-
toxin is spontaneously and rapidly de-
veloped whereby the individual is rendered
immune to the toxic and deleterious effects
of the nervous shock!

May we not conceive that under the
stimulus of the first sting and nettle of
hard truth, the nervous system of the pa-

tient produces rapidly an overplus of fighting courage—*rises to the emergency,* as we ordinarily say, and so is rendered immune against the otherwise depressing effects of full knowledge?

But whatever the theory, the fact has been brought home to me as it can only be brought home by actually trying the experiment; the fact, namely, that patients and patients' friends exhibit an astonishing power to stand the full truth, an amazing immunity against its depressing defects. No one ought to believe this who has not tried it. All that my say-so ought to accomplish is to make someone ready to try the experiment; to take the risks which we must always face if we are to get ahead, and see whether he can verify my findings.

One precaution, however, must be borne in mind. Anyone who is familiar with experimental work knows that the difficulty of verifying another's experiment is often due to failure to repeat just that experiment and no other. A certain blood-stain is highly lauded. Others try it and cannot get the results which its inventor claims for it. But very often they fail because they have not followed exactly the details of the inventor's technic.

So, if anyone tries to repeat my experiments I trust that he will notice just what it is that I recommend him to try. I am not saying that a doctor should explain to every mother in full detail the cause, symptoms, course, and prognosis of her baby's illness. I have never tried that experiment, and I should suppose it would be a very stupid, useless, and probably harmful thing to do. I do not believe in cramming information down people's throats or trying to tell them what they cannot understand properly, any more than I believe in button-holing every acquaintance in the street, and giving him a detailed account of what I consider his faults and failings.

But if my friend asks me for an opinion of his first literary productions, and if I think that they are dreadful rubbish, I do not consider it friendship to say pleasant things of his style and thereby encourage him to pursue literature as a calling. I do not give my opinion unless it is really asked for. But if it is, I do not believe in lying to save anyone's feelings. It does more harm and bruises more feelings in the end.

So in medicine, if a patient asks me a straight question I believe it works best to give him a straight answer, not a rough answer, but yet not a lie or a prevarication. I do not believe it pays to give an answer that would justify a patient in saying (in case he happened to find out the truth)—" That doctor tried to trick me." I have heard a patient say that, apropos of a lie told by one of the most high-minded and honorable physicians I know, and I do not believe it advisable for any of us to expose ourselves to the chance of rousing that sort of indignation in a patient.

A straight answer to a straight question is what I am recommending, *not an unasked presentation of any of the facts of the patient's case.* He may not care to know those facts any more than I care to know the interesting details of dental pathology in which my dentist might wish to instruct me; I prefer to leave all that to him. Just so my patient may very properly prefer to be told nothing about his disease, trusting that I shall do my best and let him know when there is anything for him to do in the matter.

But a straight answer does not mean what is often called the " blunt truth," the " naked truth," the dry, cold facts. Veracity means (as I have said) the attempt to convey a *true impression,* a fully drawn and properly shaded account such as is, as I well know, very difficult to give. I know one physician (and a splendid type of man he is, too) who, when he sees a case of rheumatic heart trouble, and is asked for a prognosis, is apt to say something like this: " Well, I'm mighty sorry for you, but your trouble is incurable. Your heart is damaged past repair and there is not much of anything to be done except to take sodium salicylate during the acute attacks and hope that the process will become arrested spontaneously before long." " Is it likely to get worse? " asks the patient. " Yes, I'm afraid that it is."

Now in one sense that is all true, but the impression that it will convey to the patient is not true, not at all what I mean by veracity. I would rather a physician would tell this sort of truncated, imperfect, and very distressing truth, than give the patient a smooth and pleasant assurance that he can be cured and that all will go right provided he does so and so.

But better than either a misleading half-truth or a pleasing lie, is an attempt so to answer the patient's question that he shall see not only what he can't do and can't hope for, but what he can do and what there is to work for hopefully. That his heart-valve is leaky and perhaps useless is true, and in that sense, to that extent, he is incurable; the damaged heart-valve is damaged once for all. Yet by accommodating himself to his diminished heart power, the patient can gradually educate to a considerable extent both his heart and the rest of himself. His heart can be made to adjust itself to its maimed state and to put forth, in spite of it, a good deal more power than it would have done without the educational process; and the individual, by learning to take the best advantage of all the power he has, can accomplish, not all that he could in health, but yet perhaps as much as he actually *would* have done, allowing for the amount of wasted time and wasted opportunity that has often to be deducted from the effective power of a healthy man.

Because this kind of explanation is so difficult and takes so much time, doctors are apt to shirk it and give the patient either a rough half-truth or a smooth lie. In our free dispensaries one can witness any day a rich and varied assortment of these two methods of shirking a difficult and tedious explanation; the rough half-truth and the smooth lie are dealt out by the shovelful and students watch and make their choice between these two pitiful makeshifts according to their temperaments, often in entire ignorance of any *tertium quid*. For it is particularly in dealing with uneducated people, such as frequent dispensaries, that we distrust the power of truth and the possibility of conveying it. In this field I have made many experiments both with lies and with the truth. I know very well that the truth is sometimes next to impossible to convey, owing to differences between the patient's vocabulary (or his habits of mind) and the physician's, but on the other hand the lie may do more harm, for there is more chance of its being implicitly believed.

To refuse to answer questions is now and then a necessity and need not involve any falsehood. For example, to balk meddling inquiries by an outsider is often our business. Then there is the patient about to undergo an operation, who sometimes catechizes us about the details of the operation, though he had better remain ignorant about it until after it is over. On the other hand, if the patient's mind is already occupying itself with a definite, but exaggerated picture of the horrors of the operation, a prosaic explanation of the real facts may act as a sedative.

Not infrequently we need to choose our time well, if a piece of painful truth has to be communicated, and it may be necessary to avoid giving the patient a chance to cross-question us at a time when we consider him temporarily below par. I have heard a patient say: "The doctor didn't mean to let me get that out of him to-day," but it was said without any bitterness or sense of being tricked by his physician, for the fact that the doctor avoided being questioned presaged that, if cornered, he would not tell a lie.

I have said that in my experience patients and their families often develop a most astonishing power to rise to the emergency and to bear the hard truth when it has to be told. But I cannot say that this is always so. There may be cases, I suppose there are such, when the patient does not react from the shock of a cruel truth, but is made worse by it. It is said that such a shock sometimes turns the scales and brings death. I have never seen this happen, but I cannot deny the possibility.

Ought we to persist in telling the truth

even when we know that it may kill the patient? Could any effect produced by a lie be as bad as the loss of a human life?

Before answering this question directly, let me ask you to consider a somewhat fanciful hypothesis. Suppose it lay in our power to let loose into the atmosphere a poisonous gas, which would vitiate the air of a whole town so that the whole community would gradually suffer in efficiency, in physical and moral fiber. Would it not be worth sacrificing a human life to save a whole community from such deterioration?

Now a lie seems to me to do something like that. By undermining the confidence of man in man it does its part in making not one but every human activity impossible. If we cannot trust one another, we cannot take a step in any direction. Business, social relations, science, everything worth doing depends on mutual confidence. It is the very air we breathe. To poison it is to do a thing far worse for society than the loss of a single life. Hence though I believe that it is extraordinarily rare to be able to save a life by a lie, it seems to me that the remedy, the lie, is worse than death.

III

Truth and Falsehood in Treatment

In discussing truth and falsehood in diagnosis and in prognosis, I have dealt chiefly with spoken truth or spoken lies. In the domain of treatment the true or false impression is often conveyed without words.

I do not know who it was that defined a quack as " one who pretends to possess or to be able to use powers (either of diagnosis, prognosis, or treatment) which in fact he knows he is without." If we think over the various forms of quacks familiar to us—Dr. Munyon, with his lifted hand swearing to the value of all those specific

cures which he knows he does not possess;
the cancer curers, those who advertise to
cure " weak men," Francis Truth, who
cheats his dupes with all-healing handker-
chiefs sent through the mails at $5 apiece
—we see that they all pretend to use
knowledge about valuable medicines or
other remedies which they know are
frauds.

Now, I was brought up, as I suppose
every physician is, to use what are called
placebos, that is bread pills, subcutaneous
injections of a few drops of water (supposed by the patient to be morphine), and
other devices for acting upon a patient's
symptoms through his mind. How frequently such methods are used varies a
great deal I suppose with individual prac-
titioners, but I doubt if there is a physician
in this country who has not used them and
used them pretty often. It never occurred
to me until I had given a great many
" placebos " that, if they are to be really

effective, they must deceive the patient.   I
had thought of them simply as a means of
getting rid of a symptom and no more a
lie than hypnotism or any other form of
frankly mental therapeutics.

But one day a patient caught me in the
attempt to put her to sleep by means of a
subcutaneous injection of water.   " I saw
you get that ready," said she, " and there
is no morphin in it; you were just trying
to deceive me."   I was fairly caught and
there was no use in trying to bluff it out,
so I merely protested that my deception
was well meant, that it profited me nothing, that it was simply intended to give
her a night's rest without the depressing
effects of morphia, etc.

" Of course I see that," she said, " but
how am I to know in future what other
tricks you will think it best to play me for
my good?   How am I to believe anything
you say from now on? "

I did not know what answer to make at

the time, and I have never been able to think of any since.

But water subcutaneously does not differ in principle from any other placebo. If the patient knows what we are up to when we give him a bread pill it will have no effect on him. If he is dyspeptic he must believe that we consider the medicine we give likely to act upon his stomach and not *merely upon his stomach through his mind.* Otherwise it will do him no good. Suppose we said to him: " I give you this pill for its mental effect. It has no action on the stomach "; would he be likely to get benefit from it? No, it is only when through the placebo one deceives the patient that any effect is produced. It is only when we act like quacks that our placebos work.

But what harm, one may ask, does a placebo do? Admitting that it is a form of deception and that if a doctor is detected in it the patient and his friends are

likely to lose confidence in him, what harm
does it do, so long as you are not found
out?

Well, as previously said, I do not think
it is a good thing for any man to succeed
only so long as he is not found out, but
there are other objections to the use of
placebos which I will next try to explain.

The majority of placebos are given because we believe the patient will not be
satisfied without them. He has learned to
expect medicine for every symptom, and
without it he simply won't get well. True,
but who taught him to expect a medicine
for every symptom? He was not born
with that expectation. He learned it
from an ignorant doctor who really believed it, just as he learned many old
legends, as, for example, that pimples are a
disease of the blood, that " shingles " kills
the patient whenever it extends clear round
the body, and that in the spring the blood
should be " purified " by this or that

remedy. It is we physicians who are responsible for perpetuating false ideas about disease and its cure. The legends are handed along through nurses and fond mothers, but they originate with us, and with every placebo that we give we do our part in perpetuating error, and harmful error at that. If the patient did not expect a medicine for his attack (say of mumps) we should not give it, yet we do all we can to bolster up his expectation for another time, to deepen the error we deplore.

Some years ago an unfortunate patient was floating around from one clinic to another, as happens now and then when diagnosis and treatment are unsuccessful. This poor woman complained that she had a lizard in her stomach, that she felt his movements distinctly, and that they rendered her life unbearable. Doctor after doctor had assured her that the thing was impossible, that no such animal could sub-

sist inside a human being, that the trouble
was wholly a fanciful one, and that she
must do her best to think of it no more.
But all such explanations and reassurances were of no avail.

One evening a group of physicians at a
small medical club were discussing the
nervous affections of the stomach, with
this case as a text. Then up spoke one
of the elder of the number had said, " I'll
fix that woman; you send her to me!" So
said, so done. The unfortunate female
appeared at his clinic within a few days.
Our friend the doctor listened with great
attention to all her symptoms, nodding his
head gravely from time to time. He entered a lengthy account of the case upon
his records, and meditated sagely for a
time when she had finished. " Yes," he
said, with a sigh, " there is no doubt about
it; it's a clear case of lizard in the stomach.
It is no use concealing the truth from you
any longer; you have every symptom of

the disease. But we have made a good deal of progress within the last few months, Madam, in the treatment of that trouble, and while I cannot make any promises (for no honorable doctor can do anything of that kind), I think I can give you good hope that you may be relieved. A medicine has recently been discovered which, in the majority of cases,—not all cases, mind you—will dissolve lizards in the stomach and allow the resulting substance to be excreted by the kidney. As I say, Madam, I cannot promise a cure, but this I can promise:—within a few days after you have taken my medicine you will be absolutely sure whether or not it has proved effective. In case it should prove effective, you will notice within forty-eight hours from the time you take it an extraordinary change in the color of your urine, which will be tinged some shade of blue, or bright green. In case the medicine fails, as is quite possible that

it may, there will be no change whatever
in the color of the urine. The medicine
will be contained in three capsules, for
which I have just written a prescription;
they can be obtained only at one apothe-
cary's in the city, as the medicine is difficult to procure and known to but few. I
have written his address on the prescription."

The doctor then handed her a prescription for three-grain capsules of Methylene
Blue, a substance which, when taken
into the stomach, invariably produces a
deep blue color in the urine. The woman
took the medicine, perceived to her amaze-
ment and delight that a blue color was im-
parted to her urine, recognized that the
lizard must have been dissolved, and was
at once freed from all her symptoms.

Now, this is the end of the story as it is
usually told; but there is a sequel. Within
the course of three months another lizard
grew. This time the poor lady had no

more faith in Methylene Blue as a permanent cure, and turned up at still another Out-Patient clinic under the charge
of a very honest physician, to whom she
told her story. He said of course that
it was ridiculous and impossible, because
lizards couldn't grow in people's stomachs.
" Oh," she said, " you know Doctor Blank,
don't you? He is a good doctor, isn't
he? " " Yes." " Well, he told me I had
all the symptoms of lizard in the stomach.
He wouldn't tell me a lie, would he? "

" Well, anyway, you haven't got a lizard in your stomach now." From this the
doctor went one step further than anyone
had gone before; he investigated not only
what was not the matter with her, but
what the trouble actually was. He found
that she had an excess of gastric juice in
her stomach, the irritation of which gave
the gnawing and scratching feeling which
she attributed to the presence of a lizard.
Having discovered this fact he proceeded

to treat her for this trouble, which he succeeded in curing, and after that time the
lizard never grew again. All of which
shows that lies do not always work, and
that the truth sometimes does.

Placebos with or without lies are unnecessary. I have for the past few years
been trying the experiment of explaining
to the patient why he does not need a
drug, when there is no drug known for his
trouble. It takes a little more time at
first, but one thorough explanation serves
for many subsequent occasions. One has
only to remind the patient of what we have
gone over with him before. When the occasion for a drug really comes, the patient
has far more confidence in its workings.

We doctors feel these things acutely
when a patient comes to us who has been
previously under the care of another
physician who educates his patients. How
refreshing to hear the mother of a child
sick with measles say, " Well, I don't sup-

pose he needs any medicine, does he? The disease has to run its course, I suppose, and nursing is the main thing." That mother has been given the truth by her physician instead of placebos, and has become accustomed to realities as easily as most people learn to believe outworn errors. Or the other hand, we see now and then a patient into whose mind it has been carefully instilled by some physician that every draught of fresh air must be avoided like a plague, that every symptom needs a drug, and that a visit from the doctor every few days is a necessity to salvation.

But the habit of giving placebos has another evil result. It gives the patient indirectly a wrong idea, a harmful idea of the way disease is produced and avoided. If symptoms can be cured by drugs, it is impossible to bring to bear upon the patient the full force of that most fundamental principle of therapeutics: " To remove a symptom remove its cause." That a man can be made well " in spite of himself " as the patent-medicine advertisements say (that is, in spite of violating the laws of health) is a belief produced as one of the by-products of the way we hand out placebos, especially in our hospitals and dispensaries. Thus we foster the patent-medicine habit.

No patient whose language we can speak, whose mind we can approach, needs a placebo. I give placebos now and then (I used to give them by the bushel) to Armenians, Greeks, and others with whom I cannot communicate, because to refuse to give them would then create more misunderstanding, a falser impression, than to give them. If I give nothing at all the patient will think I am refusing to treat him at all; but if I can get hold of an interpreter and explain the matter, I tell him no lies in the shape of placebos.

Before I close this chapter I want to speak of one further point which my ex-

periments with truth and falsehood have
brought home to me. When I have
plucked up courage and ventured to tell
the truth in hard cases, I have been surprised again and again to find how all the
chances and accidents of nature have
backed me up. Everything seems to con-
spire to help you out when you are trying
to tell the truth, but when you are lying
there are snares and pitfalls turning up
everywhere and making your path a more
and more difficult one.

I will sum up the results of my experiments with truth and falsehood, by saying
that I have not yet found any case in
which a lie does not do more harm than
good, and by expressing my belief that
if everyone will carefully repeat the experiments he will reach similar results.

The technic of truth-telling is sometimes
difficult, perhaps more difficult than the
technic of lying, but its results make it
worth acquiring.

CHAPTER V

SOCIAL WORK IN HOSPITALS; THE PALLIA-
TION OF ABSENT-MINDEDNESS

Suppose a person sharing the ideas expressed in the foregoing chapters were
suddenly and for the first time in his
life deposited in a busy hospital clinic.
Suppose also that he is a genius and can
see through his own eyes, as the rest of
us rarely do. What will most of all surprise him? Not the rush and roar of it
all. That he is used to wherever Americans are at work. Not the foul air and
bad smells. He has learned long since
that the practice of hygiene is for other
people, not for ourselves who preach it.
Not the amazing and unnecessary ugliness
of every room and hall. Rather he will
be arrested by the astonishing *absent-
mindedness* of the doctors.

The philosopher, intent upon his problem, may abstractedly walk over a precipice, but I never heard of one so absent-minded as to push a young girl over a precipice as we are doing every month in our gynæcological clinics. Not an atom of cruelty or hard-heartedness about it;—purely the habit of abstraction, the habit of saying, " My job ends here."

" She came in to find out if she was pregnant. I told her ' Yes,' and she went off. Is that pushing her over a precipice? "

Yes, in many cases it is just that. The doctor is so absent-minded that he doesn't notice the push towards hell which his word all innocently gives her. " Yes, you are now cut off from your family, who will be indignant at the shame you put upon them; from your friends, who will no longer want their names coupled with yours. You will be branded as ' fallen ' and kindly looked down on by those who have fallen perhaps far oftener than you, though in less obvious ways. Everyone in the community will be against you except the keepers of the brothels. You cannot longer go on earning an honest living, for if you try to do so, your condition will soon be observed. If you try to get square with the world again by killing your child before its birth, you will run a considerable danger of death by blood-poisoning, and the law will regard you as a criminal if you are found out. That is all to-day;—step into the next room, please, and the nurse will help you to dress."

I say—a man who in effect gives that message to a girl and *doesn't notice that he has done so* is wonderfully absent-minded. Methodically his mind has passed on to the next case, to the sterilization of his rubber gloves, to the record sheet on which he is writing his diagnosis and his account of the physical examination. He is absent-minded precisely as the mathematical professor or the philosopher is absent-minded, because his mind is so actively *present somewhere else.* The mathematician is not vague or dreamy. He is abnormally clear, but he is so concentrated and specialized upon one set of problems that he doesn't notice the rest of the world. So the doctor's mind is absent from certain human aspects of his patients' lives merely because his attention is so strongly concentrated upon disease.

Now it is always dangerous to be absent-minded. It is risky to have one's head so full of mathematics as to ignore physics and fall into a ditch, to become so absorbed in profit and finance as to allow unprotected machinery to maim workmen, to be so wrapped up in Eddyism as to catch and spread smallpox, to be so bent on good-fellowship as (absent-mindedly) to get drunk. But if ever there was a place

where absent-mindedness is dangerous to
life and limb, to soul and body,—that place
is a hospital.

Why? Because its contents are so curi-
ously assorted. People wander in there,
—the first because he has lost his money,
and the next because he has lost his mind.
The third needs a ham splint, the fourth
needs a husband (who has deserted her).
One wants a fortnight's outing, another
wants false teeth and something to put
between them. New caution with the cat
(which gives ring-worm), new care with
the cooking (which spoils digestion), new
plaster jackets and new plans of action,—
absolutely we can see no end to the variety
of need that pours in through the hospital
gates at nine and pours out again at
noon with some sort of patch or plaster
on it.

Presence of mind, presence of the whole
resources of the best-trained intellect, we
obviously need if we are to do anything for

this miscellany when once it is sorted out. But the task is made ten times harder, ten times more of a Waterloo for the absent-minded, by the fact that each need comes to us obscured under a blinding dust-storm of understatement, overstatement, misstatement, and omission. The poor folks have no idea what they need. They know that they are off the track,— that's all.

The need, then, is for all-round human beings who can supplement the necessary and valuable narrowness of the physician. The physician is there because he has learned a great deal about *one* small but vital aspect of human life,—learned it at the expense of a habit of violent absent-mindedness towards other aspects. His value, his skill, rest on this concentration of his. But with the painful acquisition of this necessary habit of abstraction he becomes a dangerous man, just as the lawyer, the orator, and the financier are dan-

gerous,—unless *supplemented and bal-
anced*. Abstractedly he will give an ap-
petizing, bitter tonic to a starving man, or
break up a family some crowded Satur-
day morning, unless there is help at hand.

II

There is a vast deal of work in a hospital
that the doctor can't do and doesn't want
to do. For example,—he has neither the
time nor the talent to teach hygiene, to fit
new sets of habits to the idiosyncrasies of
each sufferer's build. Yet without hygiene
most of medicine is useless, and without
skillful fitting to the individual's needs,
hygienic rules are simply old junk.

Better health means more money usually;—in consumption, heart disease,
neurasthenia, somebody has got to hustle
for some money if the doctor's orders are
to be carried out. He doesn't want to go
out and hustle for the money, but neither
does he care to whistle to the wind, or give

orders that can't be carried out. To order
for one patient a diet which he cannot buy,
for the next a vacation which he is too poor
to take, to forbid a third to worry when
we know that the necessary cause of worry
remains unchanged, to give the fourth di-
rections for an outdoor life which we are
morally certain he won't carry out, to try
teaching the fifth (a Jewish mother) how
to modify milk for her baby, when she
understands perhaps half of what you say
and forgets most of that,—such a morning's work is not satisfactory in the retro-
spect.

Therefore to make the doctor's work
worth while to himself and to the patient,
it must be done (in hospitals) in co-operation with someone who has time and ability
to teach hygiene and to see that it is carried out (for instance, in tuberculosis), to
study the home conditions and report upon
their part in causing or prolonging disease, and to help modify those conditions,

financial, mental, moral, which stand between the patient and recovery.

This " someone " is the social worker,—a man or woman trained to think of a human being as a whole just as naturally as the physician concentrates attention upon a part.

" What's missing here of the essentials of a human life? " asks the social worker. No matter whether her job is in a factory (as welfare worker or factory nurse), in an immigration station, in a court-room, in an almshouse, a schoolhouse, or a hospital, —her job is to supplement the efforts of the specialist in the interests of healthy, living character.

In a hospital-patient the missing necessities may be food and clothes, rest, work, decency, hope, self-respect, a bath, a crutch, or a confidant;—to make him *wholesome* the social worker looks steadfastly to the man's *whole* needs and tries to fill in wherever the need is greatest. He is *the synthesizer,* and he must stand beside the analyzing specialist always, if hospital work is to be worth the enormous sum it costs. The physician trained to special analytic keenness can give us diagnosis, but hospitals were not founded for diagnosis but for diagnosis-issuing-in-efficient-treatment.

III

As I look over the varieties of social service work which within the past four years have been established in a dozen or more hospitals in Boston, New York, Chicago, Philadelphia, Baltimore, and Cleveland, the degree of success seems to me to depend once more on the amount of team-work, that is, on the intelligent co-operation between the social workers and some physician or physicians in the hospital itself. Unless there is at least one doctor who really knows what the social worker is trying to do, the scheme fails. If he thinks of her merely as a nurse and asks of her only such help as a nurse can render, she will either fall short of his expectations (in case she has no adequate nurse's training) or will narrow herself to fulfill the purely physical needs (in which case she is not doing social work), or finally she will exceed his expectations and his horizon—which will make him think her " uppish " or interfering or visionary.

Unless a doctor has already acquired the " social point of view " to the extent of seeing that his treatment of dispensary patients is slovenly, without some knowledge of their homes, their finances, their thoughts and worries,—he will think that the social worker is trying to teach him how to do his work whenever she does what he didn't and couldn't do before. Naturally he will resent this indignantly. A doctor is treating a young girl—quite unsuccessfully—for insomnia. A social

worker discovers through a home visit that
she is sleeping (or trying to sleep) in the
same bed with two other girls,—a fact she
never would have mentioned to the doctor.
Now, if the doctor is quite unaware of
the social, financial, and psychical background out of which individual " cases " of
disease emerge momentarily (and quite
misleadingly) at the hospital, he will not
care to be advised by any " woman charity
worker." That she can throw light upon
" *his* case " implies that his vision of it was
not previously clear. The more useful she
is the more it will irritate him, if he has not
previously been led to discover that he is
attempting a task impossible without some
such aid as hers. I have seen a good deal
of such irritation implied or expressed in
the comments of physicians on social work
in hospitals, and in the long run it is sure
to checkmate the effort of the social worker
no matter how tactful she is.

It is not worth while then, in my

opinion, for any outsider or outside body
to establish social work in a hospital unless
some physician in that hospital has already become aware of his need of such
help. The doctor must first have felt
the difficulty of finishing the work which
his diagnostic studies begin or of carry-
ing into effect his desire to go to the bottom of his cases, to find their cause (physical, chemical, hygienic, financial, domestic,
emotional, or whatever it may turn out to
be) and to root it out.

The truth is, that before proper and
helpful co-operation of doctor and social
worker can be established each of the two
must educate the other considerably—perhaps painfully. The social worker must be
led to understand, for example, how often
" laziness " is a sign of disease rather than
of sin and how devious and unexpected are
the paths by which sex-tension connects
itself with cruelty, with " nervousness,"
and with slipshod habits. The doctor

must be helped to see how a patient's physical good may have to be sacrificed temporarily in order that a job may not be lost or a family broken up.

IV

But this co-operation of doctor and social worker is only one of the forms of team-work which grows up in a hospital as soon as social work is established there. My interest in its establishment springs from the perception that it involves and combines all the types of team-work which this book describes. It brings medical backgrounds and medical foregrounds into their proper organic unity. It helps medical and sociological minds to pool and exchange their earnings. It allows the teaching art to take its all-important part in the prevention and suppression of disease. Finally social workers can bring doctor and patient still closer by acting as inter-

preters, and helping on a free, full, truthful explanation on both sides.

If I can show how these various teams
are actually hitched up when social work
is established in a hospital, it will serve to
focus and summarize the meaning of this
book.

(a) I have pictured in Chapter I that
insane separation of foregrounds and
backgrounds which hospital hurry, medical routine, and scientific absent-mindedness tend to bring about. Now the social
worker is not permeated by the hospital
traditions of hurry; moreover she is to a
certain extent defended from catching the
deadly miasm of routine, by the necessary
miscellaneousness of her work, while the
very mainspring of her activity is anti-
specialism. A foreground gone astray
from its background shocks a social worker
like a runaway horse. It must be caught
and taken home. But the case-histories
piled on the desks in our dispensary clinics

are just such foregrounds torn away from
their backgrounds. No. 3861 describes
the shriveled and clammy fingers of a
" splendid case of Raynaud's disease " and
how " the case " was engaged to return on
a certain day for the professor's teaching
hour, and how the patient spontaneously
improved each summer when warm
weather limbered her useless fingers till
the return of winter renewed her sufferings. All these facts stare one in the face.
They are in the foreground.

But the background,—her life away
from the hospital—her past—her future?
Where is it? A social worker went in
search of it, ascertained that the girl had
been a good worker whenever her hands
were sound enough to be of any use,
found a place for her as a domestic in
Florida, arranged for her journey thither,
and thus gave her a winter of comfort
and self-support—her first in many
years.

(b) Teaching,—training has usually gone hand in hand with medical work in our hospitals,—teaching, that is, for everyone but the patients. Doctors, students, nurses, ward tenders, all are getting their training in most of the hospitals of this country. But the patients? How many of them are being efficiently and skillfully taught those fundamental and far-reaching lessons on which their permanent recovery often depends? We know that the cure of most cases of incipient phthisis, of neurasthenia, and dyspepsia is made possible only by a long course of training. Such patients must learn to give up lifelong habits, to acquire new ways of thinking, new self-control. But they cannot and will not make these radical changes in their lives merely because they are handed a printed list of rules prescribing how they shall eat, drink, sleep, and act. This problem the social worker attacks as an educator—all the more effectively

because she is not merely an educator but
a person endowed by the patient with some
of the authority of the hospital in which she
works, and of the physicians with whom
she is associated. To train a neurasthenic
or a tuberculous patient we need the team-
work of doctor, educator, and social
worker as described in Chapter III. Social workers in hospitals must be or become
teachers and thus make possible the triple
team-work which we need. This is very
little realized by those who think that an
ordinary nurse or an ordinary associated
charity agent, untrained for teaching and
unfitted for it by sympathy and interest,
can do social work in hospitals.

(c) All good team-work arouses my
enthusiasm. Football, part singing, ma-
chine politics, even house-breaking are
admirable so far as team-play is manifest
in them. But of all the forms of medical
team-play to which the spirit of our time
is leading us, none seems to me so fruitful,

so full of efficiency and of promise, as that in which doctor and patient get together against their common enemy—disease.

This union the social worker can do much to promote and to develop. A patient needs (for example) to be persuaded to undergo a surgical operation. The doctor has no time to explain in detail the reason why he advises this perilous venture. It is impossible for him to blow his own trumpet and expound his own fitness to advise, his own cautious weighing of the pros and cons. But if the social worker genuinely believes in the physician with whom she works, she can speak for him and help to build up in the patient that well-deserved confidence which is half the battle in medical work.

Social workers may thus help the patient to have faith in the expert. They also help the expert to have faith in the patient. The expert naturally hesitates to explain his plans of treatment to the patient because he fears that the explanation—made hastily in a noisy room to a bewildered Jew or Italian—will convey only that scrap of knowledge which is a dangerous thing. So doctors have gone on giving bread pills (encouraging thereby the habit of depending on drugs rather than on hygiene) because there was no time or opportunity adequately to explain to patients why drugs are sometimes unnecessary, how diet, fresh air, regular habits, and clean minds may work both the cure and the prevention of disease.

But with the social worker acting now as teacher and interpreter, passing on to the patient the doctor's ideas in words of one syllable, reiterating and illustrating them, following up and correcting errors of misunderstanding, it becomes possible for the doctor to deal frankly and truthfully with his patient, sharing knowledge rather than issuing arbitrary commands.

Possessing at last the *principle* of treatment, the patient can learn to apply it to himself and finally to teach others.

Can anything be more inspiring than the thought of the endless chain of helpfulness thus linked up? All over the country cured consumptives are acting as missionaries to teach other consumptives what they must do to be saved. But at the Massachusetts General Hospital this is only one of the endless chains which our team of doctor and social worker constructs. Girls who have been helped through their time of bitter trial, have borne and cared for their illegitimate children and finally married, are now helping to care for other girls in trouble like their own. They in turn will some day want to help others.

Neurasthenics who with the help and teaching of our social workers have learned to understand the doctor's ideas, to master their vagrant impulses, to " side-track " their nagging pains, to forget their fears, and to get some happiness out of life—already some of these " converted " sufferers are passing on the gospel to others.

This is team-play extended to infinity. Without exaggeration we may say that such a linkage and brotherhood of helpfulness has no end, and that as far and as fast as we can really achieve it we spread the kingdom of heaven upon earth.

FINIS